268.433
O29d
2

D0520055

Wild Truth Bible Lessons

DARES FROM JESUS 2

12 MORE Wild Lessons with Truth and Dares for junior highers

San Diego Christian College
Library
Santee, CA

Check out these great *Wild Truth* books for your junior highers and middle schoolers!

Wild Truth Journal for Junior Highers
with companion curriculum
Wild Truth Bible Lessons
Wild Truth Bible Lessons 2

Wild Truth Journal—Pictures of God
with companion curriculum
Wild Truth Bible Lessons—Pictures of God
Wild Truth Bible Lessons—Pictures of God 2

Wild Truth Journal—Dares from Jesus
with companion curriculum
Wild Truth Bible Lessons—Dares from Jesus
Wild Truth Bible Lessons—Dares from Jesus 2

Wild Truth Bible Lessons

Mark Oestreicher

DARES FROM JESUS 2

12 MORE Wild Lessons with Truth and Dares for junior highers

ZONDERVAN™
WWW.ZONDERVAN.COM

Youth Specialties

10 20 PRESS

Wild Truth Bible Lessons—Dares from Jesus 2: 12 More Wild Lessons with Truth and Dares for junior highers

Copyright © 2003 by Youth Specialties

Youth Specialties Books, 300 S. Pierce St., El Cajon, CA 92020, are published by Zondervan, 5300 Patterson Ave. S.E., Grand Rapids, MI 49530.

Library of Congress Cataloging-In-Publication Data

Oestreicher, Mark.
    Wild truth Bible lessons : dares from Jesus 2 : 12 more wild lessons with truth and dares for junior highers / by Mark Oestreicher.
         p. cm.
    ISBN 0-310-25050-1 (pbk.)
    1. Jesus Christ–Teachings–Study and teaching–Activity programs. 2. Christian education of teenagers.   I. Title.
    BS2415.O37 2003
    268'.433–dc21

                                                                        2003004626

Unless otherwise indicated, all Scripture quotations are taken from the *Holy Bible: New International Version* (North America Edition). Copyright © 1973, 1978, 1984 by International Bible Society. Used by permission of Zondervan Publishing House.

All rights reserved. No part of this publication may be reproduced, stored in a retrieval system, or transmitted in any form or by any means—electronic, mechanical, photocopy, recording, or any other—except for brief quotations in printed reviews, without the prior permission of the publisher.

Edited by Rick Marschall, Linda Bannan, and Lorna Hartman
Illustrations by Krieg Barrie
Design by Tom Gulotta
Production assistance by Nicole Davis

Printed in the United States of America

03 04 05 06 07 08/   / 10 9 8 7 6 5 4 3 2 1

o Todd Temple, whose creativity and love for junior highers inspired me to continue the *Wild Truth* line of books. It's been a great ride, Todd!

Contents

Acknowledgments

Thanks to B's Cajon Coffee Company for the perfect writing spot (caffeine, quiet, and a cool breeze). Thanks to Rick and Nicole, and the rest of the YS product team, for your skill and patience with this manuscript (Nicole gave me cheese for finishing chapters!). Thanks to Jeannie, Liesl, and Max, my amazing family.

introduction

Let's face it: God's truth really is wild! God's truth works its way into our lives like a good virus, messing up our realities, challenging our false assumptions, and convicting our inconsistencies.

And Jesus' teaching—whew! It wasn't a bunch of cutesy stories and moral platitudes. It was often in-your-face dares—dares to follow him, dares to be agents of justice, and dares to love others the way God loves us.

This last installment in the *Wild Truth* line of resources for young teens looks at 12 more dares from Jesus. In case you didn't know, it's drawn from a student book called *Wild Truth Journal: Dares from Jesus.* That student journal (or devotional) leads kids through 50 of Jesus' challenges. The two books can be used together. And, of course, since this is *Wild Truth Bible Lessons: Dares from Jesus 2,* this book has obviously a prequel. Use these books and their lessons in any order. Mix and match; pick and choose. Put together a series of lessons that will challenge your students right where they are.

Speaking of you challenging your students brings an important assumption to mind—we at Youth Specialties, and I as an author, totally believe in your ability to know your own students. In practical terms that means we trust you to modify, tweak, and mutate these lessons. Sure, if you teach them just as I've written them, they'll probably work okay with your group. But if you exercise your knowledge of your group to destroy these lessons, the impact will be much greater! Use the lessons as jumping off points. Not that you need our permission—you would do this anyway, right? But consider this *more* than permission: it's encouragement. You know your group, and we don't!

Each lesson in this book has the same basic structure—

Wanna Play? introduces the subject. It's meant to be fun (in most cases), and to pull your group together before you dive into the meat of the lesson.

It's the Truth, the second section in each session, is the Bible teaching portion. It looks at a specific dare that Jesus himself gave us (all of these are, obviously, from the gospels).

Truth in Action is a very important section. It asks (and hopefully answers) the question: What does this look like in the life of a young teen?

Take the Dare!, the final step, is a personal application—the dare part! These applications are extremely important because they give students an opportunity to respond to Jesus.

This *Dares from Jesus* series is the third and final installment in the *Wild Truth* line. The first series (a student journal and two books of Bible lessons) are simply called *Wild Truth Journal* and *Wild Truth Bible Lessons.* These look at a variety of Bible characters and the life-lessons from their stories.

The second series, called *Pictures of God* (again, a student journal and two books of Bible lessons), focuses on 50 self-portraits of God found in Scripture. Each self-portrait offers us a glimpse of God's character. And since we are made in God's image, we should be able to develop that character in ourselves also.

I am passionate about young teens (see a discussion of the importance of young teen ministry I compiled with 16 other young teen workers on the Youth Specialties site at www.YouthSpecialties.com/articles/topics/resources/soul-bolstering.php). I hope to work with them for the rest of my life. It is absolutely one of the most crucial times in life—especially for spiritual formation. My ongoing hope and prayer is that God will greatly use you in the lives of young teens, and that God will use these lessons and the time you and your group spend talking about these *Dares from Jesus* to draw kids into a more intimate relationship with their loving God!

May God richly bless you in your crucial ministry with junior highers!

Your partner in ministry,

Mark Oestreicher

Enough Said

"Again, you have heard that it was said to the people long ago, 'Do not break your oath, but keep the oaths you have made to the Lord.' But I tell you, Do not swear at all: either by heaven, for it is God's throne; or by the earth, for it is his footstool; or by Jerusalem, for it is the city of the Great King. And do not swear by your head, for you cannot make even one hair white or black. Simply let your 'Yes' be 'Yes,' and your 'No,' 'No'; anything beyond this comes from the evil one."

Matthew 5:33-37

GOALS

STUDENTS WILL—

- Understand that this dare isn't about keeping promises, but being a person whose word can be counted on
- Consider what this looks like in the life of a young teen
- Rate their own current level of trustworthiness, and choose an application for this week

SAY WHAT YOU MEAN!

Pass out copies of the opening worksheet (**Say What You Mean!**) and pens or pencils to each kid. Explain that the sentences at the top of the page are super-wordy versions of the common phrases at the bottom of the page. Have students work in small teams of two to three to match them by writing the number of the wordy version into the blank next to the corresponding common phrase.

Give them five minutes or so (not too much time—keep them a bit rushed). Then call the group back together, and go through the questions one at a time. Read the wordy sentence (if you can!), and have the students shout out their guesses of the correct translation. Then reveal the correct answer. Consider

YOU'LL NEED

- ö copies of 1.1 (**Say What You Mean!**) and pens or pencils for each student.
- ö Optional: a small candy prize for the winning team(s)

giving some sugar stimulant (a small candy bar or something) to the winning team or teams.

Here are the answers—
"Caution: apple filling may be hot long after crust is cool." *3*
"If you're going out of the house, wear clean underwear." *2*
"Look both ways before crossing the street." *4*
"Wash your hands before you eat supper." *1*

Make a transition by asking these questions. Don't offer answers yourself or correct students' responses at this point. Just surface some ideas that you'll clarify later.

- **What's the purpose of making promises?** *Theoretically, it means your word can really be trusted on that item.*

- **If you tell your friend you'll do four things, but you attach a promise to one of them, what might that mean about the other three?** *Hey, no promises! Maybe it's true, and maybe it's not—maybe you mean it, and maybe you don't.*

PLAY ON WORDS

Divide your students into larger teams (eight to 10), depending on the size of your group. If you have a small group—say six kids—then you'll have one group! Instruct the groups to turn in their Bibles (make sure each group has at least a couple Bibles) to today's dare, in Matthew 5:33-37. You read it to them:

> "Again, you have heard that it was said to the people long ago, `Do not break your oath, but keep the oaths you have made to the Lord.' But I tell you, Do not swear at all: either by heaven, for it is God's throne; or by the earth, for it is his footstool; or by Jerusalem, for it is the city of the Great King. And do not swear by your head, for you cannot make even one hair white or black. Simply let your `Yes' be `Yes,' and your `No,' `No'; anything beyond this comes from the evil one."

YOU'LL NEED

☺ Bibles or another way to make the dare passage visible for an extended period of time (the passage is too long to put on one PowerPoint or MediaShout slide).

Now tell them they have five minutes to come up with a short play based on this passage. It doesn't have to be a literal interpretation of the passage—it just needs to communicate the dare. (Note: you still haven't really explained the dare. That's okay—you'll unpack it more after the dramas.)

Give them *at least* five minutes for their creative work. But at some point, round 'em back up and have each team present its drama. Make sure you heap praise on any micron-sized amount of effort, and that no one gets teased or ridiculed (zero tolerance, baby!).

Now lead a discussion on the dare with this line of questions—

• Jesus wasn't talking about swearing, as in *cursing*—he was talking about making promises. Can someone give me an example of this kind of swearing? *I swear to you that I'll return your money.*

• But Jesus isn't really making a big deal about promises—it's not like he's saying, "I dare you not to make promises." So what do you think this dare is really about? *(This might be a tough question. It may have been clarified by one of the dramas—but it may not have been. Push your kids to think—encourage them to look at the last sentence of the passage.) Jesus wants us to be truth-tellers. When we promise some things and not others, it implies that our word can't be taken at face value all the time. The dare is: speak the truth, don't try to mislead people or manipulate them with what you say. Just speak honestly. (Note: if your kids don't get something remotely close to this in their responses, you'll want to state the dare for them.)*

• What does it look like to be someone who speaks honestly? Can you give me examples? *(Some kids might assume this is about lying—that is not the point of the dare.)*

ARE THEY TAKING THE DARE?

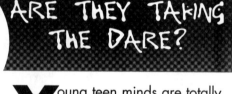

Young teen minds are totally capable of grasping this dare. However, as you could see from the line of questions above, there's ample opportunity for total confusion about what it really means. (You might be thinking, "Isn't there *always* ample opportunity for total confusion when it comes to the mind of a young teen?") This exercise is designed to clarify the dare yet again, while giving tangible examples of what it looks like in the junior high world.

Read the following short case studies, and have students vote on whether the main character is taking the dare or not. After they give a "yea" or "nay" to each situation, ask a few questions about why they voted the way they did. Check for understanding and that kind of stuff!

Use as many of these as you have time for—

Rory wants to take this dare. So when his mom asked him if he did his homework, he answered, "Mom, I swear I did it!"
(Rory pretty much missed the point, and he did just the opposite of the dare!)

Nicole wants to be someone who speaks honestly all the time. So when her friend Mindi asked her to promise that she'd keep a secret, Nicole answered, "Mindi, everything I say is a promise—you can believe what I say."
(Yup, Nic gets it.)

Terrell isn't sure he understands the dare. But he's trying. When his mom asks him if her hair looks okay, Terrell answers honestly, "It looks horrible, mom—you look like a freak! Sorry, but that's the honest truth."
(Uh, good try, Terrell. But speaking the truth doesn't mean slaying people!)

Candace is convinced that taking this dare is important. She's not going to make a big deal about it by telling everyone what she's doing. She's just going to make sure that people can count on what she says to be true—all the time.
(Candace nailed it! Four stars for Candace!)

MY TRUTH METER

Pass out half-sheet copies of **My Truth Meter** (Wildpage 1.2) and pens or pencils to each student. Ask them to take a couple minutes on their own to complete the sheet—first being totally honest about their current level of trustworthiness on their word; then reflecting on what they could do this week to put the dare into action.

After a few minutes, ask if there are a few students who would be willing to share their answers (specifically to the "what now?" question).

Then close your time in prayer, asking God for courage and strength to be people of truth, people whose word can be counted on, people who live out this dare.

YOU'LL NEED

ό half-sheet copies of **Wildpage 1.2** and pens or pencils for each squirrel, er, I mean, student

W I L D P A G E

Say What You Mean!

1.1

Each of these sentences is a wordy version of the common phrases below. Write the number of the wordy sentence next to its corresponding common phrase.

1. Proper removal of foreign organic materials from opposable digitals connected to the primary function base is required to the later planetary rotational consumption of vital nutrients while gathered in the familial tradition of voluntary communication.

2. Current and unsoiled fabric weavings worn for the biological cleanliness of certain potentially infectible areas, as well as the need for support and foundation of lesser seen, though often favored bodily regions, is needed prior to the use of both manual and automatic means of transportation that carry individuals from a communally comfortable environment.

3. Mental and physical restraint applied to warning and non-pain-oriented precognitive thoughts must be strenuously applied at this time: pulverized contents of sweet, reddish, tree-born, roundish foodstuffs could most likely, and often are, heated past acceptable pain levels, and will remain so for extended periods after the flour-based artificially sweetened containment vessel has become acceptable to human standards of pleasantness.

4. When self-transporting by means of lower appendages, exercise extreme caution by dual-ocular organs in both left and right directions; only then proceed to the opposite foundation of mechanical transportation-designated pathways.

___ Caution: apple filling may be hot long after crust is cool.

___ If you're going out of the house, wear clean underwear.

___ Look both ways before crossing the street.

___ Wash your hands before you eat supper.

14

From *Wild Truth Bible Lessons—Dares from Jesus 2* by Mark Oestreicher. Permission to reproduce this page granted for use only in buyer's own youth group. This page can be downloaded from the Web site for this book: www.YouthSpecialties.com/store/downloads   password: dares2
Copyright © 2003 by Youth Specialties.

My Truth Meter

First, put a needle on this meter to show how much you currently live out this dare. How much can people really count on what you say to be the truth—all the time, no exceptions, no exaggeration, no manipulation?

People can count on my word some of the time.

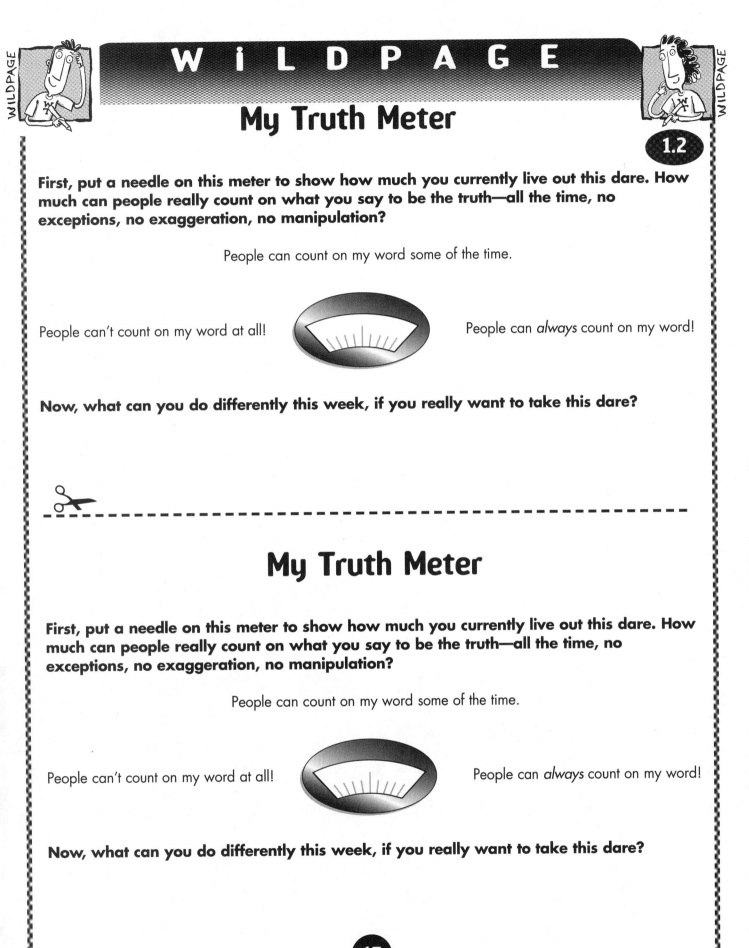

People can't count on my word at all!

People can *always* count on my word!

Now, what can you do differently this week, if you really want to take this dare?

✂ -

My Truth Meter

First, put a needle on this meter to show how much you currently live out this dare. How much can people really count on what you say to be the truth—all the time, no exceptions, no exaggeration, no manipulation?

People can count on my word some of the time.

People can't count on my word at all!

People can *always* count on my word!

Now, what can you do differently this week, if you really want to take this dare?

15

From *Wild Truth Bible Lessons—Dares from Jesus 2* by Mark Oestreicher. Permission to reproduce this page granted for use only in buyer's own youth group.
This page can be downloaded from the Web site for this book: www.YouthSpecialties.com/store/downloads   password: dares2
Copyright © 2003 by Youth Specialties.

Make it a Two-Way Street

For if you forgive men when they sin against you, your heavenly Father will also forgive you. But if you do not forgive men their sins, your Father will not forgive your sins.

Matthew 6:14-15

GOALS

STUDENTS WILL—

- Understand why forgiveness is such a big deal to Jesus
- Consider the difficulty of forgiveness in third-person case studies
- Choose a specific act of forgiveness to put into action this week

I FORGET!

Have kids work in teams for this opening game. If your group is small, your teams should just be pairs. If your group is larger, you could have up to 10 kids on a team. You make the call! Give each team a piece of blank paper and a pen, and have them choose one person on their team to be the scribe (to record their team answers).

YOU'LL NEED

- blank paper and pens (just one per team).
- Optional: small candy prize.

Explain that you'll read a short story, and then ask some questions about it. Don't offer much more explanation than this. The only rule is that they're not allowed to write anything down while you're reading the story.

After you read each story, ask the questions that go with it. Have teams write an answer. Or, if they can't come up with an answer, they should write, "I forget!" When you've completed the questions for one round, read through them a second time, and have teams shout out their answers. Those who

couldn't think of an answer shout out, "I forget!" (Note—these questions are intentionally very difficult. You want kids to be verbalizing, "I forget!")

Use as many as of these three stories as you have time for—

Round one
The villagers of Tonka-Ronka had a major problem on their hands—a troll living under their bridge that went by the name of Santerazio. Of course, none of the villagers could remember the name of the troll, so they either called it Brillitzki or Jeff. Except little Petunia—she called the troll Punky-Stocky-Fuzzy-Walla.

The villagers tried to scare the troll away with shouts of "Wahana-Goober-Fleesee-Stooble" (which was a traditional scaring technique in their village). That didn't work. They tried to scare the troll away with explosive Blastoranium—a local form of dynamite. That didn't work. And they tried painting the bridge a bright shade of the color iridescent puce, thinking the troll would just be too embarrassed to live under a bridge that color. But that didn't work either.

Finally, the little girl came up with the solution: she sat on the bridge and sang a made-up song over and over. The words were, "Cola, Cola, Here's our Troll-a. It scares our stoobles and eats our Frola. It won't come out of its stupid little hole-a; so I'll sing this song 'til it moves to Gambola." It worked! The troll got so sick of the little girl's awful, annoying voice that he moved to that other town!

Questions—
• **What was the name of the troll—the real name?** *Santerazio*
• **In addition to** *Jeff,* **what was the other name the villagers called the troll?** *Brillitzki*
• **What was the little girl's name?** *Petunia*
• **What was the traditional chant used to try to frighten the troll?** *Wahana-Goober-Fleesee-Stooble*
• **What was the name of the explosive they tried?** *Blastoranium*
• **What color did they paint the bridge?** *Iridescent puce*
• **What town did the troll finally move to?** *Gambola*

Round Two
Four friends—Genevieve, Paco, Shawna, and Arturo—decided they should start a company. Sure, they were just teenagers (the girls were 14 and the guys were 13); but they had a great idea. They would come up with names for products, from a teen's point of view.

A week later they got their first customer: a small clothing company called Stinzano Wearable Goods. The company asked them to come up with a new brand of T-shirts. They thought of Distance, Rock Wear, Diva, and Jump. But in the end, they suggested a made-up word as the brand—Bluzamato.

Whether it was a good name or not, the company loved it, and the teens started getting more work. For Shooroney Shoes, they came up with the name for the Blitz line of shoes, as well as the Creep-Off slipper

brand. **They named Carry-On notebooks for a stationery company called The Dudorf Office Goods Corporation. And finally, they were asked to come up with names for each of the five flavors in a new line of sodas made by the Blooco Soda Company. They came up with Tear-Jerker Lime, Samba Orange, Cruise Cola, Rude-Boy Root Beer, and Freakish Blue Jam. Everything was going great—until their parents made them shut down the company because they weren't getting their homework done.**

Questions—
• **What were the girls' names?** *Genevieve and Shawna*
• **What were the boys' names?** *Paco and Arturo*
• **What were two of the names they** *didn't* **use for the T-shirt line?** *Distance, Rock Wear, Diva, and Jump*
• **What** *did* **they name the T-shirt line?** *Bluzamato*
• **What was the name of the line of slippers?** *Creep-Off*
• **What's the name of the stationery company they did work for?** *Dudorf Office Goods Corporation*
• **What was the name of the soda company?** *Blooco Soda Company*
• **What was the name for the lime soda?** *Tear-Jerker Lime*

Round Three
The sign said—Welcome to the Interplanetary Travel Station. Please obey all the rules. The rules were—
   1. **Never tease a visitor from the planet Austoria-X.**
   2. **Never, ever tease a visitor from the planet Austoria-X, or you'll be sorry.**
   3. **Always dump your Gronsies at the F-43 dumping bay.**
   4. **Get back in line.**
   5. **Don't run in circles and squeal like a Plandoranium, or you will be treaseled.**
   6. **If you don't have your Fludo-10 credentials, you'll need to go to the Schtotzer's office.**
   7. **Enjoy yourself.**

8. Our restaurants and vending machines only accept money from Earth, Freedonia, and the Brofolio Alliance. Any other funds will need to be exchanged at one of the many Clam Counters.
9. Any violation of the rules will be dealt with swiftly by the Carponitus Enforcers, our Travel Station police.
10. Never forget rule number one.

Questions—
• **What dumping bay should you use to dump your Gronsies?** *The F-43 dumping bay*
• **If you run in circles and squeal like a Plandoranium, what will happen to you?** *You will be treaseled*
• **You can only use money from Earth, Freedonia, and what other location?** *The Brofolio Alliance*
• **Where can you get other foreign currency exchanged?** *Clam Counters*
• **What are the Travel Station police called?** *Carponitus Enforcers*
• **You'll have to see the Schtotzer if you don't have what credentials?** *Fludo-10 credentials*
• **And, of course, never, never tease a visitor from what planet?** *Austoria-X*

After you've played as many rounds as you have time for, have teams total up their correct answers. Consider awarding a small candy prize (or perhaps a Yak) to the winning team.

Now make a transition by saying something like this: **I heard some correct answers in that game— but I also heard a lot of that two-word phrase, "I forget!" It's pretty normal to forget details like those, since there were so many, and they had such odd names. Sometimes forgetting is a terrible thing; and sometimes it's a wonderful thing.**

Get as many responses as you can to these questions—
• **When is forgetting a bad thing?** *When you're taking a test. When you're buying Christmas gifts. When you're supposed to call home.*
• **When is forgetting a good thing?** *When you*
have a bad memory. When you need to forgive someone.

UNPACKING THE DARE

Before your group meets, recruit four people to read the parts in a reader's theater. A reader's theater is just a script with no staging. The readers simply stand in front of the group and read their assigned lines. Your readers could be students, adult leaders, or a combination of both. Just know that the impact will be greatly enhanced if you select readers who can get through their lines without much trouble. No matter who the readers are, it's best to have them read through the script a few times so they're comfortable with their lines. Also, it will make it easier for the readers if you highlight their lines (and only their lines) on their copy of the script.

At this point in your group time, ask the four readers to come to the front and read the script. Ask your group to pay close attention to what it says about forgiveness.

YOU'LL NEED

꙳ Four volunteer readers, four copies of the reader's theater script— ideally with parts highlighted.

After the performance is complete, thank your readers (*especially* if they are teens!). Then lead a discussion with these questions—
• **What were some of the reasons given for why forgiving others is so difficult?** *We have to give up what we think is our right to not forgive.*
• **Can you think of some other reasons?**
• **What were some of the reasons given for why forgiveness feels so good? Why do we want it so badly?** *Because it removes our guilt. It helps us to be whole again.*
• **Can you think of any other reasons?**
• **What, exactly, is the dare Jesus gives on this subject?** *It's Matthew 6:14-15.*
• **How do you respond to this dare?** *It's almost more of a threat!*

ONE-TO-10 FORGIVENESS

Tell your group you're going to read them half a dozen case studies where forgiveness is needed. After each one, you're going to ask them to think about how difficult it would be to forgive if they were the main character. To do this, they should hold up between one and 10 fingers to represent the difficulty. One finger in the air (be careful what finger they use!) means: "This would be a total cakewalk to forgive—no big deal!" Ten fingers means: "I'm not sure I could forgive—it would certainly be really, really difficult!"

YOU'LL NEED

- nothing (unless you use the optional idea below)

Optional idea: a little more movement

By this point in the lesson, you might be sensing your group could really use some movement (I know, you're thinking, "At what point does my group ever *not* need movement?!"). Instead of the fingers up idea, have kids move to respond. Place an *easy to forgive* sign on one wall and a *way hard to forgive* sign on the opposite wall. After each case study, have students respond by standing somewhere on the continuum between the two walls.

Ben has a difficult situation on his hands. He just found out that his best friend Marco has been stealing stuff from him. He noticed stuff like CDs and money missing from his room. But today he saw some of the stuff in Marco's room. Marco admitted it, and says he's really sorry—he doesn't know what he was thinking.

Samantha is really ticked! Her younger sister borrowed her favorite shirt and got a big stain on it. And her sister doesn't even seem sorry. She just says, "Hey, mom buys your clothes anyway. Why do you even care?"

Steven's dad has been under a ton of pressure at work lately, and he seems grumpy all the time. Tonight at dinner, Steve made a snotty comment about it, and his dad blew up at him, yelling, "I don't need this from you! You have *no* idea what real life is like!"

Shantelle was adopted as a baby—she's always known that. But she just met her birth mom; and all of a sudden she's feeling bitter about the fact that her mom didn't keep her. Her birth mom says it was because she knew she couldn't take care of Shantelle at the time.

Gary is Dustin's favorite uncle. He's always been fun and taken Dustin to do all kinds of cool things. But recently, Dustin has had an old memory come back to him. It's pretty fuzzy; but when he was a little kid, he remembers Gary touching him in some places he shouldn't have.

Carly's friend, Jesse, promised she wouldn't tell anyone that Carly liked Tommy. But she did—she told Andrew, Tommy's best friend. Jesse feels terrible about it, and keeps telling Carly how sorry she is.

It's probably a good idea—since some of these situations are really serious—to follow up this exercise with a few comments like—**Some hurts are pretty deep. And just saying, "Okay, I forgive!" isn't always enough. You might need to have someone help you work through your hurts. And sometimes, like in the case of Dustin and his uncle Gary, you should tell an adult about it.**

FORGIVENESS TIME

Can you believe it? We made it all the way to the final exercise without a handout. (Yeah, I'm big on having kids write things down—it pushes them to really process their thoughts and commit to something.)

Make copies of **Forgiveness Time** (Wildpage 2.1). Pass these out along with pens or pencils (I use golf pencils—they're really cheap and I don't get tweaked when a kid destroys one!). Ask your students to spend a minute or two in silent prayer, asking God to reveal a situation in their own lives that calls for forgiveness. Then they should take another couple minutes to answer the questions on the sheet.

Circulate around the room to see if kids need help (and if they're staying on task). Remember that for some kids, this will be a pretty easy exercise, because the grievance against them wasn't that big of a deal. But for other kids, this could bring up some pretty deep hurts that might require some follow-up from you at another time.

Take the time (at this point, or ahead of time) to fill out a sheet for yourself also. After about five minutes, read your own answers. Then, ask if a few kids would be willing to share what they wrote with the group.

Remind your group that one of the main reasons Jesus wants us to forgive people is because he loves us so much, and he knows it's not good for us to carry around bitterness and resentment toward others. People who learn how to forgive really do have happier, more whole lives.

YOU'LL NEED

👁 copies of **Wildpage 2.1** and pens or pencils for each student

Close your time in prayer, first thanking God for the constant forgiveness he gives us—forgiveness we've done nothing to deserve. Also pray for strength and courage to follow through with responses to this dare.

For Four Readers

One: Forgiveness is hard!

Two: But I want it so much.

Three: Yeah, it's hard to give, but important to get.

Four: If I gave as much forgiveness as I want, life would be different.

One: Why is it so hard to forgive?

Three: Maybe 'cause I'd rather hold a grudge?

One: Against me?

Three: Sure, sometimes.

One: Can't you just forgive me?

Three: I don't know—you really hurt me.

One: Yeah, I know.

Four: Does it make you feel better to *not* forgive?

Three: I don't know. Not really, I guess.

Four: Then why don't we forgive more often?

Two: I think it's because it means giving up our rights.

Four: What do you mean?

Two: Well, when someone does something wrong to us, we feel like we have a right to be mad.

One: To get even!

Three: To get revenge!

One: To hold a grudge!

Three: To pout!

One: To not forgive!

Two: And it's so hard to give up that right. It's hard to put that aside and get on to the forgiving part.

Four: Yeah, but if it's the other way around…

One: If I'm the one who hurt someone else…

Two: If I'm the one who needs forgiveness…

Four: I sure want it fast!

Three: I want forgiveness as quickly as possible.

Four: Because it feels *so good* to be forgiven.

One: To have my wrong stuff put into history.

Two: For that stuff to be forgotten.

Three: Forgetting—really forgetting—seems to be a part of this.

Four: Not accidentally forgetting.

Three: No, it's more like choosing to forget.

One: Didn't Jesus say something about this?

Two: Yeah, it sounds a lot like a dare!

Four: He said, "For if you forgive men when they sin against you…"

Three: "…your heavenly Father will also forgive you."

Four: "But if you do not forgive men their sins…"

Three: "…your Father will not forgive your sins."

One: Wow—that's kind of harsh!

Two: That makes it sound like Jesus won't forgive us unless we are willing to forgive other people!

One: Why would he say something like that?

Four: Maybe because it's a big deal to him?

Three: Maybe because he really cares about forgiveness?

Four: Forgiveness is at the very center of our relationship with Jesus. Without his forgiveness, we couldn't even know him.

Three: We'd be doomed!

Four: Lost!

Three: Separated forever!

One: Okay, so the dare is clear.

Two: Forgive!

Three: Forgive!

Four: Forgive!

All (in unison): Forgive!

From *Wild Truth Bible Lessons—Dares from Jesus 2* by Mark Oestreicher. Permission to reproduce this page granted for use only in buyer's own youth group. This page can be downloaded from the Web site for this book: www.YouthSpecialties.com/store/downloads   password: dares2
Copyright © 2003 by Youth Specialties.

Forgiveness Time

2.1

Whom do I need to forgive?

Why? What did they do to me?

What would it look like for me to forgive this person? Should I talk to them?
Should I talk to anyone else about it?

What difference will it make if I do forgive them?

What difference will it make if I don't forgive them?

When will I do this, and how will I go about it?

From *Wild Truth Bible Lessons—Dares from Jesus 2* by Mark Oestreicher. Permission to reproduce this page granted for use only in buyer's own youth group.
This page can be downloaded from the Web site for this book: www.YouthSpecialties.com/store/downloads   password: dares2
Copyright © 2003 by Youth Specialties.

Don't Bow To it

"No one can serve two masters. Either he will hate the one and love the other, or he will be devoted to the one and despise the other. You cannot serve both God and Money."

Matthew 6:24

STUDENTS WILL—

- Consider Jesus' teaching that money can become a master
- Understand what it looks like for a young teen to have money as a master
- Take a dare to de-master money in their lives!

WANNA PLAY?

M-O-N-E-Y MIXER

Start your time with this fun little mixer to get everyone moving around and thinking about the subject of money. (Doesn't that seem a bit weird, to force kids to think about money?)

Distribute copies of **M-O-N-E-Y Mixer** (Wildpage 3.1) and pens or pencils—or crayons or lip liner or bird feathers and vials of ink—to each student.

YOU'LL NEED

- ☞ photocopies of one page from the financial section of a newspaper (the stock listings) from more than one day, and a writing utensil for each team
- ☞ Optional: a small candy prize for the winning team

Tell them they can complete the items in any order they wish, but that they can only get a person's initials once (forcing them to actually mix).

Say "Go" and let the insanity begin. (Yeah, that's intentional overstatement—but junior high ministry is pretty regularly something akin to insanity, isn't it?)

Consider having some kind of candy or food prize for the first- and second-place competitors (maybe a jar of squid or something?).

Depending on your time frame, you can let the game continue even after the first two have finished, just so everyone gets a chance to complete most of the items.

Then ask—

- **Talk to me about money for a bit. Why's it such a big deal to most people?**

- **What kinds of things would you buy first if you had an unlimited amount of money?**

- **What kinds of things can't money buy?**

- **If you had to choose between being off-the-charts rich but really lonely, or poor but with lots of friends, which would you choose? Why?**

MY TWO MASTERS

Recruit five kids to play parts in a spontaneous melodrama. If you've never done a spontaneous melodrama before, here's how they work: it's basically a drama without rehearsal. Kids (or leaders) volunteer to play the characters, and you (or another leader) act as the narrator and read the script. The actors (I use this term very loosely!) simply play their roles as they hear them described. If they speak a line in the script, you read it first, and then they repeat it in character. It's best if you get students to play the parts who will really ham it up, and strongly encourage them to do so!

YOU'LL NEED

☺ volunteers to play the roles in a spontaneous melodrama, and Bibles

It doesn't matter if you only have five kids in your group! You don't *need* an audience for a spontaneous melodrama or role play.

This particular melodrama is set as a Ninja movie.

After the brilliant, Tony-award-winning presentation is complete, and the genuine appreciation of the spellbound crowd has subsided, thank your actors, and regroup. Distribute Bibles if your kids don't have them already (or be prepared to show the Bible verse in some other way—maybe using MediaShout or PowerPoint). Tell the group the melodrama is based on a verse in the Bible, a dare from Jesus. Have students turn to Matthew 6:24, then read the passage.

> **No one can serve two masters. Either he will hate the one and love the other, or he will be devoted to the one and despise the other. You cannot serve both God and Money.**

Now lead a discussion with these questions, or others you create—
• **What does Jesus mean that you can't have two masters? Why not?**

• **What does it mean to serve money as a master?**
• **How can you tell if money is a master to you?**
• **Be honest; give yourself a rating of 1 to 10 as to how much you care about money—1 means "I don't care about money at all" and 10 means "I'd do anything for more money."**
• **Jesus talks a lot about this subject, but Christians in countries with money (like the United States and Canada) tend to ignore these verses, or make it seem less important than other stuff Jesus talks about. Why do you think that is?**

FINANCIAL ADVISORS, INC.

Tell your group it's just become a leading consulting firm called Financial Advisors, Incorporated. They help people make decisions about how to handle money and live for only one master. Their firm specializes in advising teenagers.

If your group has 15 students or fewer, you may want to stay in one group. Or you might want to break into discussion groups, so that more kids have an opportunity to participate. If you divide (the group, that is—it's not like you're a single-cell being!),

YOU'LL NEED

☺ Nothing but your good looks and charm

it's best to have an adult leader in each group to lead the discussion once you pose the situation. Ideally, this leader will facilitate discussion but allow the students to come to their own conclusions.

Read the situations below, and then allow the students to discuss their advice. Each group (even if it's just one group!) should come to some kind of consensus about what advice it will give and have someone formally present the group's response. Of course, you don't have do use all the case studies if your time is short (as if I have to tell you that!).

Options: If you're using groups for this exercise, consider giving each group a different client, have them prepare a response, then present their client and response to the whole group.

Client #1—Jen Yen

Hi, I'm Jen Yen, and I'm writing all the way from Japan! My problem is that my dad is the CEO of a big bank here, and my parents are super rich. I know that might not sound like a problem to you. I don't need advice on what to do with all my money. I need advice on how I can not care about it when I'm surrounded by it all the time.

Client #2—Stephen Downanout

Hey, my name's Steve. I'd really like the advice of your company, but I don't think I can pay for it. 'Cause I've got, like, no money at all. I don't have a dad, and Mom has been out of work for a couple years. We get a little money from people now and then, but mostly we just scrape by on government help. My problem is, I think about money all the time! I think it's lame for people with lots of money to have any problem with it—I mean, if anyone deserves to be obsessed with money, it should be me! But I don't want to be. And I don't want any stupid simple answers, like, "Well, just don't think about it so much," or "Just be happy with what you have." C'mon, put yourself in my situation.

Client #3—Chris College

Okay, this kinda stinks. Oh, I'm Chris, by the way. I'm heading off to college in three weeks—and for a couple years now I've been planning on going into financial planning, just like your company. I really like numbers and stuff, and I know you can make a lot of money in this business. So I've got my college courses all set and

everything—I've got my whole future planned out. And now I hear that Jesus is daring me to only serve God, and not money. Well, does that mean that I have to be poor? Does that mean I can't get a job that pays good money? How can I pursue these goals and still make sure God is my only real master?

THE MONEY DARE

Pass out half-sheet copies of **The Money Dare** (Wildpage 3.2) and pens or pencils. Encourage everyone to consider this dare from Jesus to not let money become a master.

Read the sheet out loud to your students. Then spend a minute in silent prayer, to allow your students to think about their responses and what God might be asking them to do. Then give a few minutes for students to fill out the *Take the Dare!* sheet on their own.

Depending on your time and the vulnerability of your group, you may want to ask a few students share their responses. If you go this route, make sure you share your own response first—remember, you set the stage for vulnerability in your group.

Close your time with prayer, asking God to help each of you see your own heart and what place money has in it. Also ask for courage to carry out the dares you've all committed to this week.

YOU'LL NEED

ö half-sheet copies of Wildpage 3.2 and yet another writing utensil for each student (come on, if your junior high group is anything like mine, they've already destroyed the pen or pencil you gave them earlier).

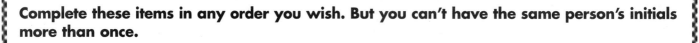

Complete these items in any order you wish. But you can't have the same person's initials more than once.

1. Bank teller. Find someone to role-play a bank teller and bank customer with you. Ask to take some money out of your account. The teller should inform you that your account is empty, and you should throw a hissy fit. Have that person initial here—_____

2. Money exchange. Either give some money to someone, or get someone to give some money to you. Have them initial here—_____

3. Raise time. Place two chairs facing one another, and find someone to sit opposite you. That person is your boss. The boss informs you that you're receiving a really big salary raise this year. You go crazy with excitement and give the boss a big hug. Have that person initial here—_____

4. Piggy bank. Sit on the floor like a little kid and pretend you're smashing your piggy bank with a hammer. Then begin to cry because there's no money in it. Have someone who saw you do this initial here—_____

5. Money cheer. Get two other people and do this cheer—
   You say, "Give me an 'M'!"
   They yell, "M!"
   You say, "Give me an 'O'!"
   They yell, "O!"
   Continue, spelling money. After the "Y"…
   You say, "What's that spell?"
   All yell, "Money! Money! Money!"
   Have them both initial here—_____

28

From *Wild Truth Bible Lessons—Dares from Jesus 2* by Mark Oestreicher. Permission to reproduce this page granted for use only in buyer's own youth group.
This page can be downloaded from the Web site for this book: www.YouthSpecialties.com/store/downloads   password: dares2
Copyright © 2003 by Youth Specialties.

The Two Masters

Cast—
Master Wa
Master Wa's Ninja Warrior
Master Cho
Master Cho's Ninja Warrior
Servant

Our story opens in the courtyard of Master Wa's house. Master Wa yells for his servant. The servant enters with his head held low, out of deep respect and fear for Master Wa. Master Wa angrily asks, "Why have you not finished your duties?"

The servant bows low and responds, "Oh, Master Wa, my deepest apologies. I will try harder."

Master Wa says, "If you do not, I will have my ninja warrior punish you!" The ninja warrior stands at Master Wa's side and executes a variety of truly frightening ninja moves.

Now we move to Master Cho's house, where Master Cho is tapping his foot with extreme impatience. He yells out, "Servant? Where are you?" The servant runs in and bows in front of Master Cho. Master Cho asks, "Have you finished your duties?"

The servant bows low and responds, "Oh, Master Cho, my deepest apologies. I will try harder."

Master Cho says, "If you do not, I will have my ninja warrior punish you!" The ninja warrior stands at Master Cho's side and executes a variety of truly frightening ninja moves.

The servant asks permission to speak. Master Cho grants permission.

The servant says, "Master Cho, you are a great and powerful master. Yet, you don't have enough money for me to be your servant alone. And so you share me with Master Wa. It is too much."

"Then," says Master Cho, "our two ninja warriors will fight to see who will have you as his primary servant."

The two ninja warriors go at it with blinding speed and spellbinding skill. They fly through the air and complete ninja moves that seem humanly impossible. The match seems perfectly even, and it goes on and on. Eventually, Master Wa and Master Cho join in the fight—two on two. Now the fighting gets even more amazing! Just when you think you've seen it all, one of the masters pulls off a move that could only be reproduced by Hollywood!

Eventually, the servant steps in and yells, "STOP!"

The two ninjas and the two masters stop and listen to the servant, who says, "This is crazy! I cannot serve two masters! I will end up hating one of you and serving the other."

The two ninjas, in their only speaking parts in this whole drama, say in unison, "The wise one has spoken."

Everyone bows to the audience, as the audience explodes into wild applause and cheers.

From *Wild Truth Bible Lessons—Dares from Jesus 2* by Mark Oestreicher. Permission to reproduce this page granted for use only in buyer's own youth group.
This page can be downloaded from the Web site for this book: www.YouthSpecialties.com/store/downloads   password: dares2
Copyright © 2003 by Youth Specialties.

I, _____ (your name), will accept the dare to not let money be my master. And I'll prove it this week by doing the following—(choose one or more)

☐ Give it away! One of the best ways to make sure we're not living for money is to give away lots of it. Not just tipping God like you would a waitress but *really* giving a lot. What will you give to this week, and how much?

☐ Ask others. Find a couple of people—maybe even one of your parents—who will be really honest with you (not just a friend who always tells you what you want to hear). Ask those people to tell you if they think money is too important to you. Then give them permission to tell you any time they see you making money a master. Who will you ask?

☐ Pray and pray. Pray about your attitude toward money. Pray that God will help you see if money is too important to you. Pray that God will help you care less about money. And pray that God will give you the courage to consider a lifestyle that doesn't allow money to become a master. When will you pray?

- -

The Money Dare!

I, _____ (your name), will accept the dare to not let money be my master. And I'll prove it this week by doing the following—(choose one or more)

☐ Give it away! One of the best ways to make sure we're not living for money is to give away lots of it. Not just tipping God like you would a waitress but *really* giving a lot. What will you give to this week, and how much?

☐ Ask others. Find a couple of people—maybe even one of your parents—who will be really honest with you (not just a friend who always tells you what you want to hear). Ask those people to tell you if they think money is too important to you. Then give them permission to tell you any time they see you making money a master. Who will you ask?

☐ Pray and pray. Pray about your attitude toward money. Pray that God will help you see if money is too important to you. Pray that God will help you care less about money. And pray that God will give you the courage to consider a lifestyle that doesn't allow money to become a master. When will you pray?

From *Wild Truth Bible Lessons—Dares from Jesus 2* by Mark Oestreicher. Permission to reproduce this page granted for use only in buyer's own youth group. This page can be downloaded from the Web site for this book: www.YouthSpecialties.com/store/downloads   password: dares2
Copyright © 2003 by Youth Specialties.

Look in the Mirror First

"Do not judge, or you too will be judged. For in the same way you judge others, you will be judged, and with the measure you use, it will be measured to you. "Why do you look at the speck of sawdust in your brother's eye and pay no attention to the plank in your own eye? How can you say to your brother, `Let me take the speck out of your eye,' when all the time there is a plank in your own eye? You hypocrite, first take the plank out of your own eye, and then you will see clearly to remove the speck from your brother's eye."

Matthew 7:1-5

GOALS

STUDENTS WILL—

- Understand what it means to judge people
- Consider why Jesus doesn't want us to judge others
- Address times in their own lives when they've judged others

YOU BE THE JUDGE

Begin with this game to get the idea of judging on the table. You can play this simple game a lot of ways. I'd use the MediaShout or PowerPoint version (similar to the Screen Play games sold by Youth Specialties—check 'em out, they're really fun with young teens!) described in the sidebar.

YOU'LL NEED

○ Either copies of **Wildpage 4.1** and pens or pencils, or the stuff for one of the handout-free zone options in the sidebar

But the more traditional way to play is to make copies of **You Be the Judge** (Wildpage 4.1). Then give students the Wildpage and pens or pencils. This is a great team activity that fosters community rather than isolation. Have kids work together in teams of four

or five to come up with a team response to each lawsuit.

Handout-Free Zone!

- MediaShout or PowerPoint game. This opening came out of a PowerPoint game I used with my own junior highers. It's ideally suited for this use. Put each lawsuit on a slide, and have students work in teams to write *real* or *fake* on a blank piece of paper for each. Then go through the lawsuits again and have the groups yell out their answers. Have the correct answer (Real or Fake) pop up over the lawsuit.
- Ultra-low-tech game. It wouldn't be the end of the world to skip the handouts *and* the high-tech stuff on this one. Just read the lawsuits to your group. In teams have them use blank paper to write *real* or *fake* for each lawsuit. Proceed through the content two times, as described in the PowerPoint game explanation.

After you've given students a few minutes to record their answers, read through the list and have teams shout out their answers. Then reveal the correct answer. Award a thousand points for every correct answer, and consider tossing small candy prizes to the team with the most points at the end. The bonus case is an opportunity for you to level the playing field a bit. Have teams add up their points prior to the bonus case. Then designate points for the bonus case to still allow multiple teams to win.

And the answers are…

• **A client filed a $2,000 lawsuit against a dating service claiming he was introduced to the wrong woman.** *Real*
• **A man sued his ex-girlfriend for $2 million due to the emotional distress caused by her breaking up with him.** *Fake*
• **A woman is suing for $475,000 in damages from a store, claiming she was permanently injured when a six-pack of beer fell on her foot.** *Real*
• **A man is suing a supermarket chain because one of its promotions offered so many bargains he hurt his back carrying them.** *Real*
• **A woman sued the United States government for $50 million—after her husband's disappearance—for "covering up his alien abduction."** *Fake*
• **A man named William Ford sued the Ford Motor Company for the continuous use of his name.** *Fake*
• **A man appealed his 18-month jail sentence, claiming the trial was prejudiced because the judge fell asleep through parts of the testimony.** *Real*
• **A woman sued her former landlord for $50,000, claiming her rented apartment was infested with bugs and that a cockroach lived in her ear for almost one week.** *Real*
• **National Aeronautics and Space Administration (NASA) was hit with a lawsuit by three men who claim ownership of planet Mars.** *Real*
• **A million dollar lawsuit was filed against Purina on behalf of a 3-year-old golden retriever, claiming the food led to the dog's laziness.** *Fake*
BONUS CASE
• **A man sued a minor-league baseball team after being distracted by the team's mascot and getting hit by a foul ball.** *Real*

Make a transition by asking these questions—
• **What's a judge's job?** *To make decisions, to decide what's fair (in accordance with the law).*
• **What does it mean to judge people?** *To make decisions about them, to conclude that they are justified, or that they are wrong.*

STORYBOARD

Divide your group into teams of about five to eight kids (smaller if your group is small). This isn't a competition, so the group size is really only important for participation reasons. Make blank paper (regular old copier paper is okay, but something a bit larger would be better) and markers available. Also have Bibles available in case any of the groups don't have them.

YOU'LL NEED

⏺ blank paper (large paper would be best), markers, and Bibles

Tell the groups that in the movie-making process, one of the first steps is to storyboard the script. This involves creating a drawing for every camera angle, dialogue point, and scene part. These drawings are simple, without much detail. This method works out the film's story before the expensive process of filming begins.

Explain that each team will function as a storyboarding group for today's dare passage. The teams turn the dare into a story and create storyboard drawings to tell the tale.

Now give them the dare passage: Matthew 7:1-5. Teams can create a literal retelling of the passage or create a short story of its own. Tell the teams they have about seven minutes to complete their storyboards. This comically visual Bible passage should create some interesting storyboarding from your group!

Circulate around the room among the teams to make sure they're staying on track (and that they're working on the right passage). It's possible your kids will need more than seven minutes for this exercise—so monitor their progress, as well as your time frame. Make sure you give them a two-minute and one-minute warning, so they know when they need to be finished.

Now pull the group back together and have each team present its storyboards. Make sure everyone pays attention when the teams make their presentations—teams shouldn't still be working on their own presentations. Also make sure you give lots of affirmation to every team, even if they show only the slightest bit of effort!

After the teams finish their presentations, debrief that passage a bit more—

• **So who can tell me what they think the Dare From Jesus is today?** *Don't judge people (duh).*

• **Why do you think God cares about this?** *God's goal for us is to love each other. When we spend our time and energy judging each other, we don't notice the stuff in our own lives that needs work, and we create divisions with other people.*

• **People outside the church often say the number one reason they don't go to church is because Christians are so judgmental. Why do you think we are quick to judge others? Why do we ignore this dare so often?** *This is one of the clear teachings of Jesus that Christians ignore more than almost any other of his teachings. We often ignore it because we think (wrongly) that it's our job to help Jesus know who's sinning or who doesn't deserve his grace!*

• **How might the world be different if all Christians really practiced this dare, all the time?** *Wow.*

WHAT'S JUDGING LOOK LIKE?

Pass out copies of **What's Judging Look Like?** (Wildpage 4.2) and pens or pencils to each student. The sheet is fairly self-explanatory—students add a needle to the judging meters to indicate whether or not the character is judging people wrongly. Just between us chickens, the characters are *all* wrongly judging others. And the exercise of rating them is a bit silly in many ways—if they're judging, they're judging. But this exercise will likely create some good opportunities for discussion in your group. If the kids just had to say "yes" or "no", you might miss the opportunity to see which characters they think are kinda judging, as opposed to those who are huge, awful, terrible judges.

Your students will enjoy this more if you allow them to work in pairs and trios.

After teams finish their ratings, make sure to spend a chunk o' time on debriefing. Ask questions like—**How many of you ranked Pammy as one of the worst judges on the page? Why? Who did you rate really high? Who didn't you think was as bad a judge as the others? Why?**

End with questions like these—**If all these teens are judging others, does it really matter who's doing it more and who's doing it less? Why or why not?**

YOU'LL NEED

ö copies of Wildpage 4.2 (**What's Judging Look Like?**) and pens or pencils for everyone

I'M JUDGING

Ask your group to take a minute to look over the characters on the **What's Judging Look Like?** Wildpage. Tell them to insert their own names in place of the characters, and see if they sound true at all. In other words, are any of the judging examples on that page examples of ways *I* have judged people?

Then ask your students to think of other situations in their lives right now where they're judging someone or a group of people.

YOU'LL NEED

ó Something for kids to write on—it could be the back of the last Wildpage, blank paper, or 3 x 5 cards.

Now direct them to some blank writing surface. Tell them to write the name of a person or group of people they're currently judging. This will be a very easy question for some of your students. For others (especially the younger students) it's a bit abstract. Unless they were paying good attention during the rest of the lesson, they might have a difficult time thinking of a personal application. It would be extremely helpful if you could give a couple examples of your own—maybe one person you've judged recently (c'mon, we all do this!) and one group of people you've judged recently.

Now ask students to think about whether or not they need to make repairs. In other words, if they've hurt a specific person, maybe an apology needs to be made or a situation needs to be corrected. Have them write a sentence or two about this.

Finally, ask the group to write a statement of commitment to choosing to move away from a judging spirit, in obedience to this dare from Jesus. Ask students to sign that statement, as if it were a contract.

Ideally, you'll spend some time in your group having various students share what they've written. You'll have to be the judge (ha!) on whether or not your group can handle that.

Wrap up your time in prayer, asking God to give group members the courage to move away from judging, and the sensitivity to notice when they're judging. Thank him for forgiving us for all the times we've judged people!

You've just been appointed to be a judge! Your first day on the job has a full ledger of cases. It's your job to decide which cases are real legal cases and which are fakes. After you read each case, write *real* or *fake* on the line next to it.

_____ A client filed a $2,000 lawsuit against a dating service claiming he was introduced to the wrong woman.

_____ A man sued his ex-girlfriend for $2 million due to the emotional distress caused by her breaking up with him.

_____ A woman is suing for $475,000 in damages from a store, claiming she was permanently injured when a six-pack of beer fell on her foot.

_____ A man is suing a supermarket chain because one of its promotions offered so many bargains he hurt his back carrying them.

_____ A woman sued the United States government for $50 million—after her husband's disappearance—for "covering up his alien abduction."

_____ A man named William Ford sued the Ford Motor Company for the continuous use of his name.

_____ A man appealed his 18-month jail sentence claiming the trial was prejudiced because the judge fell asleep through parts of the testimony.

_____ A woman has sued her former landlord for $50,000, claiming her rented apartment was infested with bugs and that a cockroach lived in her ear for almost one week.

_____ National Aeronautics and Space Administration (NASA) was hit with a lawsuit by three men who claim ownership of planet Mars.

_____ A million dollar lawsuit was filed against Purina, on behalf of a 3-year-old golden retriever, claiming the food led to the dog's laziness.

BONUS CASE

_____ A man sued a minor-league baseball team after being distracted by the team's mascot and getting hit by a foul ball.

35

From *Wild Truth Bible Lessons—Dares from Jesus 2* by Mark Oestreicher. Permission to reproduce this page granted for use only in buyer's own youth group.
This page can be downloaded from the Web site for this book: www.YouthSpecialties.com/store/downloads   password: dares2
Copyright © 2003 by Youth Specialties.

4.2

Add a needle to each of the judging meters to show how much the character is judging. 1 = no, this isn't judging; 5 = this is violating the dare big-time!

When Pammy passes a homeless person, her first reaction is always—that lazy person just needs to get a job.

Tyler is in advanced-placement classes at school. He never says mean things about kids who aren't, but does think he's somehow better than everyone else.

Grant insists he isn't a racist. "It's just," he says, "that the Asian kids at my school are so annoying!"

Kelli is sure that homosexuality is gross to God. So she can't stand even being near someone who seems gay.

James is really into worship. When other kids in the youth group just stand there during the worship times, James thinks they're really unspiritual.

Hannah agrees with her parents: anyone who doesn't go to a Christian school has their priorities wrong.

AJ has learned that it's safe to assume that anyone who smokes is really ignoring God.

From *Wild Truth Bible Lessons—Dares from Jesus 2* by Mark Oestreicher. Permission to reproduce this page granted for use only in buyer's own youth group.
This page can be downloaded from the Web site for this book: www.YouthSpecialties.com/store/downloads   password: dares2
Copyright © 2003 by Youth Specialties.

Choose Your Destination

"Enter through the narrow gate. For wide is the gate and broad is the road that leads to destruction, and many enter through it. But small is the gate and narrow the road that leads to life, and only a few find it.

Matthew 7:13-14

GOALS

STUDENTS WILL—

- Understand why this is the granddaddy of all dares, the big kahuna, the mega-dare!
- Consider what it looks like for young teens to choose "the narrow way"
- Write out the implications of making this choice for their own lives

WANNA PLAY?

CHOOSE OR LOSE!

Begin by writing a random number from one to 11 on a piece of paper (so no one can see you), and then fold it up and keep it in a pocket.

YOU'LL NEED

- ☉ copies of the Wildpage 5.1 (**Choose or Lose!**) and pens or pencils for your kids.
- ☉ Optional: candy prize

Tell your students you're going to ask them a series of either-or questions. Each question will have an *A* answer and a *B* answer. On their Wildpage, they should start with their pen or pencil at the star up top; and with each question, draw a line down the *A* or *B* channel. At the end of the series of questions, they'll end up in a numbered box. Anyone who ends up in the box corresponding with the number you've written on the piece of paper in your pocket wins!

Now, read these questions, and have students mark their papers accordingly—

1. Would you rather (a) rent a movie and stay home to watch it, or (b) go out to the theater to see a movie?
2. Would you rather (a) watch four hours of golf on TV, or (b) watch four hours of bowling on TV?
3. Would you rather (a) live on an ice-covered mountain, or (b) in a heat-scorched desert?
4. Would you rather (a) swim with sharks, or (b) wrestle a bear?
5. Would you rather (a) be the inventor of Squirt-Cheez, or (b) be the inventor of Spam?
6. Would you rather (a) be a sewage-plant worker, or (b) be a circus elephant cleaner?
7. Would you rather (a) lose the use of your legs, or (b) go deaf?
8. Would you rather (a) take a really long time to make a good decision, or (b) make a quick decision and live with it?
9. Would you rather (a) play a role in a TV commercial about constipation, or (b) not be in a commercial at all?

10. Would you rather (a) be super-emotional all the time, or (b) never experience emotions at all?

After you read all the questions, ask students to shout out the number of the box their choices landed them in (try to use the word *choices*—as this exercise is a set-up for a lesson on choices!). Tell them the numbers don't really mean anything, but that you have a random number between one and 11 in your pocket, and whoever is in the box that matches your number wins (or gets candy; or gets the new car behind curtain number two!).

With great dramatic flair, slowly pull the piece of paper out of your pocket, unfold it, and reveal it. Acknowledge those whose choices happened to land them on the winning number. Consider giving out a small candy prize to the winners. Theoretically, about 10 percent of your students should win (unless your group defies all mathematical predictability—which somehow seems like a group of young teens!).

To wrap up this time say something like this—**We have to make choices all day, every day.** Then ask these transition questions—
• **What was unique about the choices you just made in that game?** *This question might not be as simple as it seems. The choices in that game were all completely hypothetical, or "what ifs." They gave no sense where anyone would have to live out the consequences of any of those choices.*
• **How are we normally affected by the choices we make?** *This is somewhat of a rephrasing of the last question—just to make sure they get the point. Normally our choices have implications or consequences—results.*

THE BIGGEST CHOICE

Begin this section with a discussion based on these questions—
• **Some choices in life are pretty little—some are pretty big. What are some of the big**

choices? *Career, Marriage, stuff like that.*
• **What do you think the single, biggest choice in life is?** *Don't judge their answers. Rather, allow some discussion, if there is any. If multiple answers arise, consider having students vote on two or three of them. From the perspective of this Scripture passage (and this lesson!), choosing the narrow way or the broad way is the most important choice of life.*

If something like *choosing to follow God* or *becoming a Christian* doesn't surface as one of the answers to the last question, say something like—**I want to propose that choosing to become a Christ-follower is the single biggest choice you'll make in life.**

YOU'LL NEED

☺ Bibles (or a way to display the main passage), two signs—one that says "small risk, small implications" taped to a wall in your room, and one that says "huge risk, huge implications" taped to the opposite wall.
☺ Optional: a large tanker truck filled with Madagascar cinnamon.

Have students read (either by passing out Bibles or making the passage visually available) today's dare from Jesus in Matthew 7:13-14 ("*Enter through the narrow gate. For wide is the gate and broad is the road that leads to destruction, and many enter through it. But small is the gate and narrow the road that leads to life, and only a few find it.*")

Ask—**Where is the dare from Jesus in these verses?** *It's an implied dare. Jesus dares us to choose the narrow way—the path that very few choose—to choose life.*
Then—**Why is this such a big deal? What's daring about it?** *This is really important; many of your kids (and many Christians in general) don't see Christianity as a daring choice, because they're not really living as Christ-followers. They might go to church and believe in God, but that's not the kind of risky, radical living Jesus refers to—the kind that leads down the narrow path to experiencing real life. (If your students don't get somewhere close to this answer, you should clarify this point.)*

Now have everyone stand up. Point out that you've taped two signs to the walls in your meeting space.

One sign should say, "small risk, small implications," and the sign on the opposite wall should say, "huge risk, huge implications." Make sure your students know what *implications* are (it's not a common young teen word!)—the results of any choice—good or bad.

Tell them you'll read a list of big-time decisions. All of these decisions have risk or implications. For each one, you want them to move so they're standing somewhere between the two signs to show whether they think the choice has bigger or smaller risks and implications. After you read each phrase and students move, ask this set of questions—
• **Why do you think this is a big or small choice?** (You might direct this to a specific student.)
• **What might the specific implications of this choice be?** *Don't let your kids off easy on this answer. Make sure they're really thinking through how this choice will affect their lives. This is really the point of this group of questions. Other big-time choices—even those with potential life-ending implications—don't have the same weight as a life truly submitted to God has. That choice—when taken seriously—has implications for literally everything else we do in life and death!*

Here's the list—
• **Choosing whether or not to bungee jump off the world's highest bridge.**
• **Choosing which classes to take in high school.**
• **Choosing if you'll get married, and who you will marry.**
• **Choosing whether or not to dye your hair orange.**
• **Choosing whether or not you'll try drugs—just once.**
• **Choosing if you'll wear clothes to school tomorrow or not.**
• **Choosing how long you'll continue to live with your parents or guardians before moving out on your own.**
• **Choosing a career.**
• **Choosing whether or not you will really follow Jesus—living every moment of your life completely for him and not for yourself.**

Make sure you spend some time on this last question (since, uh, it's pretty much the whole point!). Then, after you call the students back to their seats, take another

minute to recap the main point again. Explain that a life that is truly devoted to Jesus—total radical discipleship—is the best way to really experience life. But not many people are willing to choose this level of commitment, which is why Jesus says it's a narrow road and few find it.

NARROW WAY ADVENTURES, MARKETING DEPT

Divide your group into groups of about six or seven (of course, if your group is six or seven kids—or fewer—then just don't divide!).

Tell each group that they are the marketing department of a company called Narrow Way Adventures. Their task is to create a one-minute commercial to convince viewers to take this dare. The commercial must deal with the actual world that young teens live in and involve one or more characters. Tell them you'll time the commercial, and they'll be cut off after one minute.

Give the groups about five to 10 minutes to put together their commercials—which, of course, will be acted out live. It would be great if you had an adult leader to help out in each group—not to tell them what to do, but to guide them and keep them on track.

After the preparation time is over, have each team perform its commercial. Make sure (this is important with young teens) to have all the other groups pay attention when it's not their turn. This doesn't come naturally to teens—they'll want to be whispering about their own commercial, especially if they haven't performed it yet. Also make sure you give every group lots of affirmation and applause.

YOU'LL NEED
◌ Nuttin'.
◌ Optional: a small panel of judges and a prize for the winning team

You might want to consider asking a panel of judges

(adult leaders or parents) to come in and judge the commercials based on creativity, use of the group participants, and message. Then award some kind of prize to the winning team (like a bag of mini candy bars).

WHAT'S IT MEAN FOR ME?

Pass out copies of **What's It Mean for Me?** (Wildpage 5.2) along with pens or pencils for everyone. They may, of course, still have pens or pencils if you used the opening handout. Instruct your students to take a few minutes on their own to write some thoughts in response to the questions. Tell them the whole thing is kind of a waste of time unless they are willing to be honest about what this choice looks like.

After several minutes (or whenever your group seems to have devolved into total chaos), pull them back together, and ask if any students are willing to share what they wrote. As said in other places, you'll greatly amp up the responsiveness of your kids if you set the pace by reading your own somewhat vulnerable written responses (you know what I mean by *somewhat vulnerable*, right? Like, it wouldn't be appropriate for you to say, "Living on Narrow Way Lane—for me—would mean I'd need to cut back on my crack addiction. How 'bout you kids?").

Of course, the implied action here is that kids would choose one or the other of these possibility sets. The problem with forcing a choice at this point is that most decisions made in a youth group teaching setting like this, in response to this kind of discussion, will most likely be contrived. It's almost counter to the magnitude of the decision you're discussing. Instead, I suggest encouraging your students to take their sheets home and spend some time this week thinking about this choice. If, during the week, they are convinced they want to walk "Narrow Way Lane," they should take a marker or pen and circle what they wrote in that section of the page. Encourage them to leave the sheet out in their room somewhere where they'll see it and be reminded of this choice.

Close your time in prayer, asking God for courage to take the path that so few choose to walk.

Optional idea: if your group has any kids who might have never chosen to become Christ-followers, this is a perfect lesson to explain the gospel and offer some kind of response. Or, if you know one or two in your group who haven't made this choice, you may want to meet with them in the week following this lesson to talk more personally about what it would mean for them.

YOU'LL NEED

- ☉ copies of **Wildpage 5.2** and pens or pencils for everyone.
- ☉ Optional: You might want to have some background music (not too rowdy) to keep distractions down while kids write.

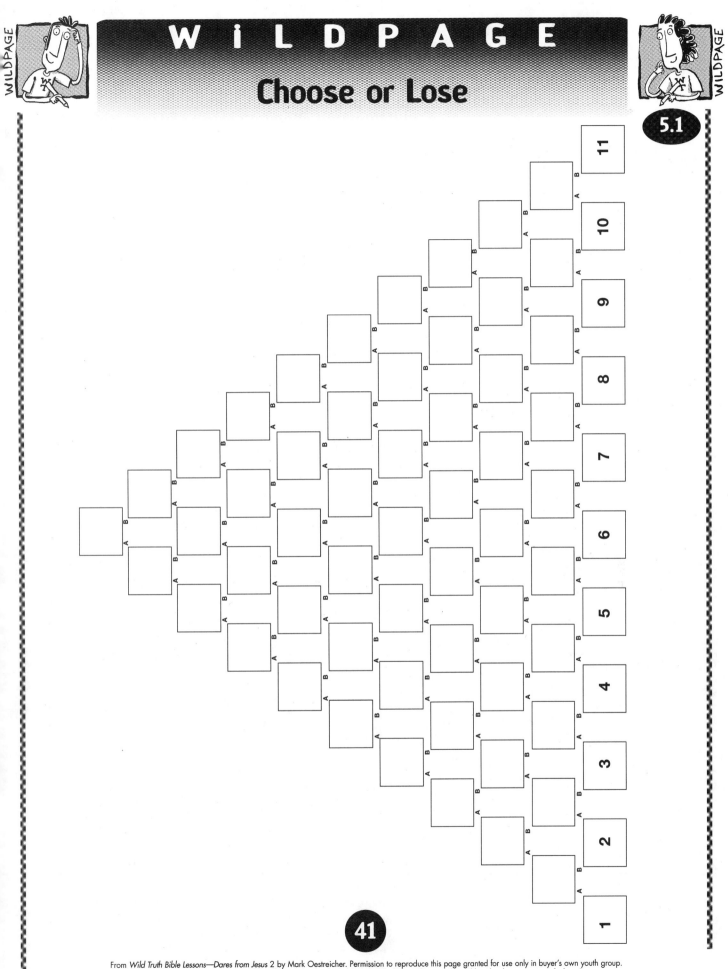

From *Wild Truth Bible Lessons—Dares from Jesus 2* by Mark Oestreicher. Permission to reproduce this page granted for use only in buyer's own youth group.
This page can be downloaded from the Web site for this book: www.YouthSpecialties.com/store/downloads   password: dares2
Copyright © 2003 by Youth Specialties.

Wide Way Boulevard

What would it look like for me to live here? How would my life be different than it is now (honestly)? And why is this such an easy choice?

Narrow Way Lane

What would it look like for me to live here? How would my life be different than it is now (honestly)? And why is this such a hard choice?

42

From *Wild Truth Bible Lessons—Dares from Jesus 2* by Mark Oestreicher. Permission to reproduce this page granted for use only in buyer's own youth group.
This page can be downloaded from the Web site for this book: www.YouthSpecialties.com/store/downloads   password: dares2
Copyright © 2003 by Youth Specialties.

Give Your Whole Heart

Hearing that Jesus had silenced the Sadducees, the Pharisees got together. One of them, an expert in the law, tested him with this question: "Teacher, which is the greatest commandment in the Law?" Jesus replied: "'Love the Lord your God with all your heart and with all your soul and with all your mind.' This is the first and greatest commandment."

Matthew 22:34-38

GOALS

STUDENTS WILL—

- Consider what it means to love God
- Talk about different ways teens can express their love for God
- Choose a *loving God* plan of action for this week

WHAT DO WE LOVE?

Divide your group into teams. The size of the team depends on the size of your group. If you have about 10 kids, you could just use a group of girls and one of guys. If you have a larger group, keep the teams to about 10 each, at the most.

YOU'LL NEED

- blank paper (small and large) and stuff to write and color with.
- Optional: small candy prizes.

Give each team a blank piece of copier paper or loose-leaf paper and a larger piece of paper (poster size would be great). Also give them a pen or pencil, and make markers or crayons available (but don't pass them out).

Tell the teams to take a few minutes to find as many things as they can that they *all* love. Each item on the list must be something that every person on the team can say, "I *love* that!" If only one person doesn't love it, they can't include it on their list. They should try to find at least 20 things they love in common.

Then they should choose the strangest one, the one thing they all love that is unlikely to be on any of the other teams' lists. Now they should work together to draw a big picture of this item on the large piece of paper, using the colors you've made available.

After another couple minutes, have the teams present their drawings to the whole group. Don't allow mocking or teasing. Make sure every team feels supported (but feel free to have fun with this process!). Consider tossing out small candies to any team with a unique "We love it!" item.

WHAT THE BIBLE SEZ...

Pass out copies of **What the Bible Sez...** (Wildpage 6.1) and pens or pencils to each student. Tell them the topic of today's dare (loving God). Explain that the handout has a bunch of Bible verses on it, some real and some fake. Their job is to choose which are which.

YOU'LL NEED

ᵔ copies of Wildpage 6.1 (**What the Bible Sez...**) and pens or pencils for everyone.

They can work in pairs if they want to.

Give your group about five minutes to finish reading through the verses and choosing the real ones.

Enter the Handout-Free Zone!

This exercise works very well without handouts—especially if you use MediaShout or PowerPoint. Create a slide for each verse (real and fake), and ask kids to decide whether it's real or fake. They could make a note of their answer, and you could go over the list a second time, revealing the correct answers. Or they could just shout out their answers.

After about five minutes, go through the list of verses, read each one out loud, and have kids shout out their answers. Pause to ask a few debriefing questions before you reveal the correct answer on each verse. If some kids guessed that a verse is fake (whether it is or isn't, in reality), ask why they think it's fake. In other words, what does the verse say that doesn't line up with what God would say to us about loving him? For verses that everyone guesses are real, reveal that their answer is correct, and then ask what the verse says to us about loving God.

Here are the real verses, with their references—
• **Love the LORD your God with all your heart and with all your soul and with all your strength. These commandments that I give you today are to be upon your hearts. Impress them on your children. Talk about them when you sit at home and when you walk along the road, when you lie down and when you get up.** *(Deuteronomy 6:5-7)*
• **But be very careful to keep the commandment and the law that Moses the servant of the LORD gave you: to love the**

LORD your God, to walk in all his ways, to obey his commands, to hold fast to him and to serve him with all your heart and all your soul. *(Joshua 22:5)*
• **This is love for God: to obey his commands.** *(1 John 5:3)*
• **Hearing that Jesus had silenced the Sadducees, the Pharisees got together. One of them, an expert in the law, tested him with this question: "Teacher, which is the greatest commandment in the Law?" Jesus replied: "'Love the Lord your God with all your heart and with all your soul and with all your mind.' This is the first and greatest commandment.** *(Matthew 22:34-38)*

Here are the fake ones, with their problems—
• **To love God is to be religious. If you are not religious, how can you say you love God? This is the very least you can do.** *Loving God is not about religion or being religious.*
• **If you desire wealth and prosperity, one thing is required of you: to love God. For if you love God and only God, untold riches will be granted to you.** *Loving God doesn't "get you stuff." It's not a deal maker.*
• **Loving God is exclusively a feeling, a reality deep in your heart. This is God's great hope, that you would feel this way.** *Loving God is much more than a feeling—it must show up in action, or it's not real love.*

ARE THEY DARE-TAKERS?

TRUTH IN ACTION

Ask for five volunteers to come to the front of the room. Explain that they really won't have to do anything—they'll just be representing characters you'll talk about. It would be best for your group to hang name signs around the necks of these five kids with the following character names (so they can remember the stories you'll read): Chris (could be a guy or a girl), Nikki, Terrance, Jasmine, and Jake.

Read these descriptions of kids trying to put this dare into action. After each one, ask students to talk about whether or not this character is taking the dare or not.

Then, after you've read and quickly debriefed all five characters, ask your group to place the five in order from "taking the dare the least" to "taking the dare the most." Move the volunteers around in the lineup to represent their rankings. Ask your students why they ranked the characters as they did.

Here are the five descriptions—

YOU'LL NEED

ö nothing. Optional: signs to hang around five kids' necks with the characters' names below.

Chris wants to love God more. So Chris is committing to saying, "I love you God" at least five times a day. Chris believes this will help him (or her) think about God more all throughout each day.

Nikki thinks talk is cheap. She wants to put this dare into action. She thinks the best way to love God is to love other people. So she's developing a friendship with a lonely girl at school who doesn't have any friends.

Anytime Terrance thinks about how he can love God more, he ends up struggling with guilt about his relationship with his parents. He's totally disrespectful to them, and he acts like a selfish jerk all the time. Terrance decides that in order to love God, he needs to obey what God says about loving his parents.

Jasmine is big-time into music. And recently she found she likes to write songs. So this week she decided that a great way to show her love God is to write songs for him. She doesn't know if anyone will ever sing them—they're just her way of expressing her love for God.

Jake wants to love God. He thought one of the best ways to do this would be to give up something he really likes for God. So he sold his BMX bike (which was pretty tricked out), and gave all the money from the sale to an inner-city mission that helps homeless people.

LOVING HIM

Pass out half-sheet copies of **Loving Him** (Wildpage 6.2) and pens or pencils. If you previously used pens or pencils, most of the boys will have certainly destroyed them by now.

Have students spend a couple minutes on their own, looking over the list of "Loving God" ideas. Ask them to choose one idea, and then write a plan of action for how they'll put it into practice this week.

Encourage them to make their plans

YOU'LL NEED

ö half-sheet copies of Wildpage 6.2 (**Loving Him**) and pens or pencils.

detailed and concrete—something they'll actually carry out.

After a few minutes, see if a few kids would be willing to share their responses. Then close in prayer, thanking God for his amazing love of us, and expressing your love for him.

Which of these are real Bible verses about loving God? After each of the fake verses, write what's wrong with its teaching.

	Real!	Fake!
Love the LORD your God with all your heart and with all your soul and with all your strength. These commandments that I give you today are to be upon your hearts. Impress them on your children. Talk about them when you sit at home and when you walk along the road, when you lie down and when you get up.	☐	☐
To love God is to be religious. If you are not religious, how can you say you love God? This is the very least you can do.	☐	☐
But be very careful to keep the commandment and the law that Moses the servant of the LORD gave you: to love the LORD your God, to walk in all his ways, to obey his commands, to hold fast to him and to serve him with all your heart and all your soul.	☐	☐
This is love for God: to obey his commands.	☐	☐
If you desire wealth and prosperity, one thing is required of you: to love God. For if you love God and only God, untold riches will be granted to you.	☐	☐
Hearing that Jesus had silenced the Sadducees, the Pharisees got together. One of them, an expert in the law, tested him with this question: "Teacher, which is the greatest commandment in the Law?" Jesus replied: "'Love the Lord your God with all your heart and with all your soul and with all your mind.' This is the first and greatest commandment.	☐	☐
Loving God is exclusively a feeling, a reality deep in your heart. This is God's great hope, that you would feel this way.	☐	☐

From *Wild Truth Bible Lessons—Dares from Jesus 2* by Mark Oestreicher. Permission to reproduce this page granted for use only in buyer's own youth group.
This page can be downloaded from the Web site for this book: www.YouthSpecialties.com/store/downloads   password: dares2
Copyright © 2003 by Youth Specialties.

Loving Him

6.2

Consider these ways to show love to God. Choose one to put into practice in the next 48 hours, and write a plan of action describing what and when and how you'll carry it out.

❏ Spend time talking to God

❏ Show some love to someone in the name of God

❏ Obey God in an area of your life where you've been disobeying Him

❏ Spend time getting to know God better in the Bible

❏ Give some money to God's work

❏ Spend time worshipping God

❏ Write a prayer or poem to God

❏ Other:

✂ -

Loving Him

Consider these ways to show love to God. Choose one to put into practice in the next 48 hours, and write a plan of action describing what and when and how you'll carry it out.

❏ Spend time talking to God

❏ Show some love to someone in the name of God

❏ Obey God in an area of your life where you've been disobeying Him

❏ Spend time getting to know God better in the Bible

❏ Give some money to God's work

❏ Spend time worshipping God

❏ Write a prayer or poem to God

❏ Other:

From *Wild Truth Bible Lessons—Dares from Jesus 2* by Mark Oestreicher. Permission to reproduce this page granted for use only in buyer's own youth group.
This page can be downloaded from the Web site for this book: www.YouthSpecialties.com/store/downloads   password: dares2
Copyright © 2003 by Youth Specialties.

Start at the Back

For whoever exalts himself will be humbled, and whoever humbles himself will be exalted.

Matthew 23:12

GOALS

STUDENTS WILL—

- Understand the concept of humility as the Bible talks about it
- Consider what real humility looks like in the life of a young teen
- Write a prayer to God expressing their desire to grow and change in this area of their lives

ME FIRST!

Before your group meets, arrange chairs (if you don't normally use chairs), and place them in rows, like a standard school classroom. If you have a small group (10 or less kids), still try to find a way to have at least two rows—or just modify the game.

YOU'LL NEED

⚬ chairs placed in a formal arrangement with rows.

Tell the kids you'll make a statement; and if it's true about them, then they have to move the number of seats you've said. If someone is in that seat, they should sit on him. Warn them to be nice to each other (if any little punk boy squawks about a large girl sitting on him, smack him upside the... wait, I mean, don't let him get away with it). Tell them that if more than one person is already in the seat, they should just stack up! Note: some of your kids will love this, and others will be way uncomfortable with it. Perfect!

Also tell them that all of the rows (side-to-side, and front-to-back) are continuous loops. So if they are supposed to move two seats to the right, and there's only one seat to their right, they should loop back to the other end of the row, and count that as the second seat. If you have a very large group (150 or more), you may want to modify this last rule, and just have kids bounce back off the ends of rows. It can add a lot of time to have people running around to the other end of rows.

You've probably played this game before, and called it Seat-Shifter or Move-About or Stack 'Em Up or something like that. You'll use it today as a learning game to introduce the idea of humility. One of the issues with teaching on this subject is to get buy-in. If you began a lesson on humility by asking, "How many of you have lacked humility?" you'd probably get a bunch of blank stares and one or two nervous half-raised hands. And if you followed up with, "What does it look like for a young teen to lack humility?" Well, more blank stares and a few confused responses. But this game accomplishes two great things—first, it gets everyone to admit, in a non-threatening way, that they've lacked humility once in a while. And it also suggests a dozen ways this might show up in the life of a young teen.

Here's the list of instructions—

- **If you've ever taken cuts in a line, move two seats to the right.**
- **If you've ever thought you were better than someone else, move three seats to the left.**

• If you've ever said the words, "me First," move one seat backward.
• If you've ever said something mean about another person, move four seats to the right.
• If you've ever been sad because someone didn't notice something you did well, move four seats to the left.
• If you've ever wanted special treatment—something no one else would get—move one seat forward.
• If you've ever wished you were famous, move three seats to the left.
• If you've ever—*ever*—acted arrogant or stuck-up, to anyone, move one seat to the right.
• If you've ever daydreamed about what it would be like to be born into a rich and powerful family, move one seat backward.
• If you've ever thought you weren't treated fairly, move four seats to the left.
• If you've ever called someone a *loser* (to their face or behind their back), move one seat to the right.
• If you've ever lacked humility, return to your original seat.

Make a transition by acknowledging that everyone in the room has lacked humility from time to time, and we might as well admit it. Also mention that the items that got them to move might be examples of that lack of humility in their lives.

IT'S THE TRUTH — OPPOSITES

Divide your group into teams for creating small dramas, the size of the teams to correspond to the size of your group. A small group might want to use one team. A mid-sized group could use teams of five to seven. A larger group might want teams of a dozen or so. The larger your teams, the more helpful it is to have an adult volunteer in each of them to guide, suggest, or boot.

Explain to the teams that you'll give them about seven minutes to come up with two *very* short dramas—like, one or two minutes each. The first sketch should show a teenager who is *not* humble. And the second should show the same teenager, in the same situation, being humble.

Of course, you haven't spent much time defining humility at this point. That's okay. Some of the dramas might be a bit off-course, but that will give you fodder for future discussion.

YOU'LL NEED

ⓞ nuttin' but Bibles

Give the teams about seven minutes to create their little works of art. Adjust the time if necessary. If you don't have adult volunteers in the groups, circulate around the room to make sure the groups are actually doing something!

Then have the groups come to the front and perform their two dramas. Give them lots of affirmation and grace—especially if they have showed even an ounce of effort. Don't allow other groups to talk and plan their skits while groups perform.

Then have students turn in their Bibles to this session's dare—Matthew 23:12 (*"For whoever exalts himself will be humbled, and whoever humbles himself will be exalted."*). Then have a discussion about biblical humility based on these questions or others you add—
• **So what *is* humility?** *Technically, it's a lack of pride. It's putting others first. And it's understanding our need for Jesus.*
• **Our world tells us to look out for number one and to put yourself first. How does this match up with Jesus' dare to us?** *It doesn't. It's just the opposite of what Jesus says!*
• **Is pride always bad? Why or why not?** *No, there's a kind of healthy pride also. This is a bit tough for kids to understand, and you might need to clarify it for them. Good pride doesn't compare to other people or wrongly puff itself up. Bad pride is all about being better than someone else or being selfish.*
• **How can you stand by a belief, with strength, and still be humble?** *This isn't an easy question, and it may take a bit of time to answer. You might have to give an example, like: What if you choose*

to stand up for a truth you believe in, like that God is real, when a teacher in history class says that religion is really something people made up because they need something to believe in? How can you make your beliefs known without coming off as arrogant?

• **Name some ways Jesus lived out this humility when he was here on earth.** *He was born in a barn! He lived as a normal person, not a rich or powerful person. He always put other people's needs before his own. And, ultimately, he took on the humiliation of being beaten and dying on the cross so he could offer us real life!*

• **Why is this idea of humility so hard for us to live out?** *We want people to notice us! We want to be valued, and it's easy to wrongly think that putting others' needs before our own will somehow take away our worth.*

• **Why do you think this humility stuff is so important to Jesus?** *He loves us and wants the best for us, and he knows that ultimately we will experience a richer life and be happier if we're not always trying to put ourselves first.*

THE GOOD, THE BAD, AND THE UGLY

One of the issues with teaching the abstract concept of biblical humility to mostly concrete-thinking teens is that they tend to adopt blanket positions. In other words, pride is either all bad or all good. And if they decide it's all bad, then the opposite must be all good. And in some of their minds, the opposite would be self-condemnation (a word they use *all* the time!) and self-loathing. Enough young teens are already there, really. So I'm trying to be careful to give you a lesson that won't end sloppily. That's why this exercise exists.

Before your group meets, make a sign that says, "Good Pride" and affix it to a wall in your room (ideally, where two semi-clear walls face each other). Affix a sign that says, "Bad Pride" on the opposite wall. These terms may seem simplistic or reductionist to you, but they'll be a helpful clarifier (I predict) for your teens. And the whole exercise can just be fodder for a

good discussion, even if you have a freakishly intelligent kid who objects to the either-or nature of these choices.

Now have your group stand in the space between these two signs, and explain that they're standing on a continuum (most will know this word from math class). Tell them you'll read some short descriptions of teens that have pride, and they should move toward one wall or the other to register their opinion. Being a continuum, they can also express the degree or intensity of their response by where they stand.

Here are the descriptions—

> **Julio's soccer team just won the regional championship. He is very proud to be on this great team. He doesn't rub it in people's noses or anything; it just makes him feel great to think of how his team pulled together.**
>
> **Shannon got second place in the science fair at school. She actually wears the ribbon around school now, and she has jokingly asked kids in her science class to call her *the professor*.**
>
> **Sarah has worked really hard this year to bring up her grades. When her report card came out, she was so excited to see all *A*s and *B*s, she ran all the way home to show her mom.**
>
> **David doesn't say anything prideful at all, ever. He's a really quiet kid. But he spends a lot of time thinking. And one of the main things he thinks about is how other kids aren't as mature as him.**
>
> **Corbin is the first-chair trumpet player in the band. He really is fantastic at**

YOU'LL NEED

☺ a sign on one wall that says, "Good Pride", and a sign on the opposite wall that says, "Bad Pride", and a second set of signs (not on the walls yet) that say, "Humility, Jesus Style" and "Not Really Humility."

playing the trumpet. He's constantly asking the other trumpet players if they'd like his help. The words he uses don't sound prideful; they sound helpful. But Corbin loves the fact that everyone knows he's the best.

Now have your kids stay standing, while you (or another volunteer) run and affix two new signs to the walls: one that says "Humility, Jesus Style" and "Not Really Humility." Read these descriptions—

Mindi tries really hard in school, and does pretty well. But it never matters how good her grades are, she still thinks she should do better and that everyone else is smarter than she is.

Cameron was chosen as Student of the Month at school. He was excited to come home and tell his parents. But his brother found out that day that he got accepted by the college he was hoping for. So Cameron decided his own news could wait another day or two, so his family could celebrate his brother's news.

Sasha is a shockingly talented singer, and she gets asked to sing solos at church and school all the time. People always give her compliments. But Sasha's attitude is, "This is a gift God gave me. I'm going to use it, but I'm not going to start acting or thinking like a celebrity or something."

Curtis doesn't even try—at anything. He can't stand it when kids he knows get all stuck-up about stuff they're good at. So he's decided to just be lousy at everything he does!

Have your group return to their seats, and wrap this section by giving a mini-talk based on this idea—
Here's the key to this Jesus-style humility. Everyone in our world is always telling us that we have to think of ourselves as **winners. We have to be confident in ourselves and think highly of ourselves. But we know the truth: without Jesus, we are totally and completely lost. And any good in us is a gift from God. So we don't waste our time either puffing ourselves up or wallowing in self-pity. Instead, we need to realize that we are all losers! Everyone is! That God cares so much about us losers that he died for us and calls us his children—that's what gives us both humility and hope!**

WHICH ARE YOU?

Pass out copies of **Which Are You?** (Wildpage 7.1) and pens or pencils to each student. Read through the description at the top of the page, which basically explains two oversimplified personality types: prideful and self-deprecating. Challenge kids to check one box or the other. They might not like characterizing themselves in one of these two ways. Remind them that checking a box just means they have a tendency in this direction. It would help if you revealed your own inclination.

Then read the next little instruction on the sheet to your students, and have them write prayers to God, expressing their thoughts about what they've learned and how they'd like to change.

Ideally, you would end your time by having students get into small groups and read their prayers aloud as a closing prayer time. If your group is small, you could do this together, with you leading the way by reading your own prayer first. You'll have to make the call as to whether your group can handle this kind of self-disclosure.

YOU'LL NEED

⊙ copies of Wildpage 7.1 **(Which Are You?)** and pens or pencils for each student

Most of us have a personality that leans to one of two extremes. Either we lean toward being prideful people—we notice everything good about ourselves and want everyone else to notice these things also. Or, we lean toward thinking terribly of ourselves all the time, believing we aren't worth anything at all, even to God.

If you had to pick one or the other to describe yourself, which would you be (you can't pick one in the middle)?

❏ **prideful**   ❏ **low self-image**

Neither of those extremes is what God wants for us! He wants us to be humble, while realizing that we have great worth to him! Write a prayer to God in the space below that expresses your thoughts about this to God—

From *Wild Truth Bible Lessons—Dares from Jesus 2* by Mark Oestreicher. Permission to reproduce this page granted for use only in buyer's own youth group.
This page can be downloaded from the Web site for this book: www.YouthSpecialties.com/store/downloads   password: dares2
Copyright © 2003 by Youth Specialties.

Believe It

"I tell you the truth, if anyone says to this mountain, 'Go, throw yourself into the sea,' and does not doubt in his heart but believes that what he says will happen, it will be done for him. Therefore I tell you, whatever you ask for in prayer, believe that you have received it, and it will be yours."

Mark 11:23-24

GOALS

STUDENTS WILL—

- Understand the dare from Jesus that we exercise more faith
- Consider what it looks like for a young teen to exercise faith
- Choose an area of their lives where they need to exercise more faith and write a prayer to God

BELIEVE IT OR NOT!

Distribute copies of **Believe It or Not!** (Wildpage 8.1) and something to write with. Tell your group you're going to test their beliefs a little—not their beliefs in God, but in other things.

The Wildpage is a list of 30 statements. Many of them are true, but some are quite fake. For each statement students should either check the box for "I believe this!" or the box for "I don't believe this!" It's more fun if you let students to work in pairs, or even small teams, rather than individually.

Give students a few minutes to fill out the sheet. Then read each statement out loud, and have students respond by shouting either "I believe

it" or "I don't believe it." Then reveal whether the statement is real or fake. Have students total their correct answers, and consider awarding some kind of small prize—like a mini-candy bar or a coupon for free accounting lessons from the church accountant (ooh! Fun!).

The fake statements are—4 (there's not even such a language!), 8, 10, 12, 17, 21, 22, 23, 24, 27, and 28. Yes, I made these up; so you've had a small glimpse into my twisted mind.

Optional variations—

- Active option—put an "I believe it!" sign on one wall and an "I don't believe it!" sign on the opposite wall. Read the statements one at a time, and have students move to one wall or the other to register their responses.
- Team option—if you have a larger group, play this in teams of eight to 12 students, and have each team come up with one answer for each statement. Don't bother using the Wildpage if you go this route—just give each team one blank piece of paper and a pen so one person can record the

YOU'LL NEED

- copies of Wildpage 8.1 (**Believe It or Not**) and pens or pencils. (Note options below that do not require use of the handout.) Optional: a small candy prize for the winner and runner-up (just what you need—kids on a sugar-buzz!).

team responses and keep score.

• MediaShout or PowerPoint game—this would be easy and fun to convert into a visual game using MediaShout or PowerPoint and a TV or projector. Simply put each statement on a slide, and have teams or individuals record their answers on a piece of paper before you reveal the correct responses.

Note: whatever variation you use, just make sure the "I believe it" and "I don't believe it" responses are part of the game, because this exercise is meant to be an opener to the idea of belief and faith. Okay? We got a deal? Don't make me come find you!

REPHRASE IT

Begin with a transition discussion based on the activity you just completed. Use questions like these—

• **What does it mean to believe something?** (Don't let your kids get away with using the word *believe* in their definition!)

• **What do belief and guessing have to do with each other?** (In that game, beliefs were based almost completely on guessing—or at least a guess based on common sense.)

🔆 Bibles, blank paper, and pens or pencils

• **How does it work to believe in something you've never actually seen, like God?** (Consider sharing an example here— ask if anyone has ever seen wind. A few might say they have, but challenge them on this. We don't actually *see* wind—we see the results of wind, and we know it's present. This is often how we *see* God.)

• **What's the difference between faith and belief?** (You could argue this different ways. They really aren't very different and to say they are is just semantics. But it's probably fair to at least say that belief is just in your head, but faith isn't faith unless it's acted upon.)

Distribute Bibles (or make the key passage available through another means, like passing out copies or projecting it using MediaShout or PowerPoint), and read the key passage—the DARE—for this lesson: Mark 11:23-24 ("I tell you the truth, if anyone says to this mountain, 'Go, throw yourself into the sea,' and does not doubt in his heart but believes that what he says will happen, it will be done for him. Therefore I tell you, whatever you ask for in prayer, believe that you have received it, and it will be yours."). Deliver a mini-talk (two to five minutes) on the meaning of the passage. Use the notes in the sidebar if you'd like.

Comments on Mark 11:23-24

In this passage, Jesus challenges us to stretch our faith. He uses an interesting word picture: that anyone with enough faith can command a mountain to toss itself into the sea. There are a couple of leading interpretations for this passage, but neither is what your students will likely assume.

A couple possible interpretations—

• Jesus was standing on the Mount of Olives, just next to Jerusalem, when he said this. He may have been using the mountain he was standing on as an example. On a clear day, one could see the Dead Sea from his vantage point—so the mountain and the sea were objects the listeners could see at that moment.

• Another interesting possibility is this—Herod, the ruling authority over this area, and one of the wealthiest and most powerful men in the history of the world, had constructed a mountain fortress just south of Jerusalem. It was called Masada, and the ruins remain there today. The amazing thing about Masada was that it was built on a mountain that did not previously exist. Herod wanted a fortress atop a mountain, so he had a mountain built. It would be an impressive feat even today—but was truly remarkable in his time, and a real show of Herod's power and control. Herod, of course, was quite oppressive to both Jews and Christ-followers. Standing on the Mount of Olives, Masada would be the only other mountain in clear view, along with the Dead Sea. It's quite possible that Jesus was telling the disciples, "Look, if you have faith, you can have even more power than Herod."

• Either way, there's not doubt that Jesus was speaking metaphorically, encouraging the disciples to understand God's power that was available to them—and to us.

What your kids will think—

Growing up in the church, I always thought it was sad that no one that I was aware of, in the history of the world, had ever had enough faith to actually toss a mountain into the sea—just to do it. I knew this verse was encouraging me to have more faith; but I also thought it was literal. And to think anything else seemed like it was proving the point—that I really didn't have enough faith. This verse (or my understanding of it) made me feel like a spiritual loser. Many of your pre-abstract-thinking students will initially have the same response to this passage. Help them understand that Jesus isn't holding up the finger-and-thumb loser sign to his forehead, and telling us to straighten up and fly right. Instead, he's daring us to stretch our faith and draw on the confidence God can give us.

Now pass out blank paper and writing stuff (some of you would like to simply pass out at this point). Ask students to work in groups of two to four to rephrase the passage. Remind them that Jesus was standing on a mountain, looking at a sea when he said this. How might Jesus have issued this dare if he were standing in the junior high world of their town?

Give the groups three to five minutes to work or until they implode and begin wreaking destruction on each other and the fine appointments of your junior high group meeting space. Ask each group to share its paraphrase. Make sure to encourage every remotely serious attempt. Teasing or belittling any real effort will teach kids to not bother trying next time.

A note about paraphrasing Scripture

Whenever I suggest paraphrasing Scripture as an exercise, I imagine some readers may have a coronary and write me off as a heretic (go ahead, I dare ya). They think things like, "The Bible clearly teaches that we shouldn't change even one jot or tittle!" (You don't hear the word *tittle* very often these days, do you?) Chill. Take a laxative. Think of it this way: you're asking (or I'm asking) your students to write biblical commentary—not to change the inspired Word of God. Okay? Breathe deeply, and continue teaching.

Wrap up this time by asking this question—**Okay, just so we're clear—what's the dare from**

Jesus in this passage? *Of course, the dare is to exercise faith more often and more completely.*

Before your group meets, write the following character names on six pieces of paper or cardstock (one name per sheet)—
- Jenny
- Sam
- Josh
- Carissa
- Jordy
- Faith

Punch holes in the top corners (or use tape) and attach string (or floss or rope or spaghetti) to make a sign that can be worn around the neck.

Now recruit six volunteer students (ideally, three girls and three boys—although you could change any of the character names other than Faith in order to reflect your volunteer gender mix). Have each volunteer wear the appropriate name sign around their necks, so they are easily identifiable—this will be important so your group can remember who's who after their stories are read.

YOU'LL NEED

ö Six volunteers to read a paragraph each. Signs to hang around their necks with their character names on them.
ö One copy of the *Rank 'Em!* stories found at the end of this lesson, cut into strips.

Make a copy of the *Rank 'Em!* stories at the end of this lesson, and cut it into strips along the lines so you have six individual stories. Hand these out to your six volunteers. Have them all stand in front of your group—wearing their signs—and read their stories.

After they finish, lead your group in an exercise to move the six characters into a line in order from "fulfilling the dare the least" to "fulfilling the dare the most." Make this an interactive time of getting lots of opinions from your group. Ask questions like—

- **Which of these characters do you think is living out this dare the best? Why?**
- **Which is living it out second best? Why?**
- **Which is living it out the least?**
- **Which completely missed the point?**

See if you can get some kind of unanimity about the overall ranking. If your volunteers are sharp enough, consider having them defend themselves or offer a rebuttal to their ranking (in character).

Large group option—

If your group is more than about 30 or 40 students, it may be difficult to get enough involvement from everyone. So break your group into smaller clumps of about 10 kids each. Give the groups blank pieces of paper and pens, and have them work as teams to rank the characters. Have each group reveal its answers and explain its reasoning.

MY MOUNTAIN, MY SEA

Distribute half-sheet copies of **My Mountain, My Sea** (Wildpage 8.2) and pens or pencils to your squirrels—I mean, students. Ask them to take a few moments of silence to think and pray about an area or two in their lives where they've been lacking in faith. You might consider playing some quiet music during this time to decrease distractions (like that wonderful 12-year-old boy who just loves to pass gas during every prayer time).

YOU'LL NEED

⌐ copies of **Wildpage 8.2** and pens or pencils for everyone

After a couple minutes, ask them to write down what they've come up with, and write a prayer to God for more faith. It would be best if you filled out a sheet also.

After a few more minutes, ask if a few students would be willing to read their written prayers during a group prayer time. Select volunteers ahead of time, and then begin your time of prayer. Set the stage for vulnerability by reading your prayer first. Don't wimp out and say something like, "God, I'm really spiritual already, but want to have enough faith to be an *even better* example to these kids!" Show some struggle!

I believe it! I don't believe it!

❏ ❏ 1. Rubber bands last longer when refrigerated.

❏ ❏ 2. Peanuts are one of the ingredients in dynamite.

❏ ❏ 3. There are 293 ways to make change for a dollar.

❏ ❏ 4. There are 78 words for *tears* in the Naganak language.

❏ ❏ 5. A shark is the only fish that can blink with both eyes.

❏ ❏ 6. There are more chickens than people in the world.

❏ ❏ 7. Two-thirds of the world's eggplants are grown in the state of New Jersey.

❏ ❏ 8. If three million people jumped at exactly the same moment, in the same square mile, it could knock the earth off its axis.

❏ ❏ 9. On a Canadian two-dollar bill, the flag flying over the Parliament building is an American flag.

❏ ❏ 10. Penguins can do back flips.

❏ ❏ 11. No word in the English language rhymes with month, orange, silver, or purple.

❏ ❏ 12. The first swim caps were made from the outer layer of a jellyfish.

❏ ❏ 13. All 50 states are listed across the top of the Lincoln Memorial on the back of the $5 bill.

❏ ❏ 14. Almonds are members of the peach family.

❏ ❏ 15. Winston Churchill was born in a ladies' room during a dance.

❏ ❏ 16. Maine is the only state whose name is just one syllable.

❏ ❏ 17. Cola mixed with squid ink is strong enough to dissolve concrete.

❏ ❏ 18. Los Angeles' full name is "El Pueblo de Nuestra Senora la Reina de los Angeles de Porciuncula."

❏ ❏ 19. A cat has 32 muscles in each ear.

❏ ❏ 20. An ostrich's eye is bigger than its brain.

❏ ❏ 21. The term *politician* comes from the Latin word for wind.

❏ ❏ 22. It takes more energy to blink one million times than to run one mile.

❏ ❏ 23. The first mass-produced candy was meat-flavored.

❏ ❏ 24. George Washington's middle name was Lester.

❏ ❏ 25. A dragonfly has a life span of 24 hours.

❏ ❏ 26. A goldfish has a memory span of three seconds.

❏ ❏ 27. The record for speed-reading the Bible is one hour, three minutes and 10 seconds.

❏ ❏ 28. The South American leaping turtle can actually jump about two feet in the air.

❏ ❏ 29. The average person falls asleep in seven minutes.

❏ ❏ 30. In England, the Speaker of the House is not allowed to speak.

From *Wild Truth Bible Lessons—Dares from Jesus 2* by Mark Oestreicher. Permission to reproduce this page granted for use only in buyer's own youth group.
This page can be downloaded from the Web site for this book: www.YouthSpecialties.com/store/downloads   password: dares2
Copyright © 2003 by Youth Specialties.

Copy this page and cut it into strips. Give each strip to one of your six volunteers to read to the group.

Jenny

Hi, I'm Jenny, and here's how I'm taking this dare—The other day, our youth pastor challenged us to reach out to someone who needs love. This really doesn't come naturally to me. But I've decided to be friends with this girl in my school who just moved from some other country and doesn't speak English very well. Everyone treats her like she doesn't even exist. And I might get teased for being nice to her. But I'm exercising faith that God will help me have the courage to follow through with this.

Sam

Hey, my name's Sam, and here's how I'm taking this dare—See, my family is pretty messed up. My dad lives with us once-in-a-while—but then he'll take off, and we won't see him for a few months or even a couple years. And my mom can't seem to keep a job because she's never on time and always complains like crazy. My sister is into drugs and stuff, and pretty much has nothing to do with our family except living in our house. So, I'm deciding to exercise faith that God will take care of me, that he'll be the father I need (since my real dad isn't a father to me), and that he'll help me to not be as messed up as my parents when I grow up.

Josh

Hi, I'm Josh, and here's how I'm taking this dare—I've got this huge test in my science class on Monday, and I'm not ready for it at all! If I'm going to pass the test, I should probably study all weekend long. But there's tons of fun stuff to do this weekend, and I really don't feel like studying. So, like tossing a mountain into the sea, I'm going to exercise faith that God will help me know the answers to the test questions even though I'm not studying. See? That takes real faith!

Clarissa

Hi, my name is Clarissa, and here's how I'm taking this dare—All my life I've loved singing, and I've planned on pursuing a career as a professional singer. And I know that God could totally use me in that area. But recently, I was totally blown away by God's command that we be active in seeking justice. And I heard about this organization that helps free child slaves and teenage prostitutes in other countries. So I'm exercising faith by choosing to go for a career as a lawyer so I can join this organization and help these people in other parts of the world. It all feels pretty risky to me, but I think this is what God really wants me to do.

Jordy

Hey, Jordy here. I'm not messing around with this dare. I'm going to really live it out. I figure if Jesus said it, then I should do it! So, there's this mountain near my house (well, it's not really a mountain—more like a hill), and a sea at the bottom of it (well, not really a sea, but more like a pond). I'm going to spend my summer vacation moving the mountain, one rock at a time, into the sea. I'm hoping that by the end of the summer, you'll be able to see a real difference in the size of the hill and the water level of the pond. Pretty cool, huh?

Faith

Yeah, my name is Faith, and I'm talking about faith—don't give me a hard time about it, okay? Here's the deal—I figured maybe I should start living out my name, you know? I mean it seems kinda dumb to have the name Faith, and be a person with, like, no faith at all. So here's how I'm going to live out this dare (this is kind of hard to admit): For a long time, I've really struggled with gossip. I just love it. My friends all call me the gossip queen—and they know that I'm the best source for getting the real info on anyone. But I need to give this up—I need to turn it over to Jesus and ask him to help me stop. It's going to be super hard. But I'm choosing to exercise the faith to loose my gossip queen title.

60

From *Wild Truth Bible Lessons—Dares from Jesus 2* by Mark Oestreicher. Permission to reproduce this page granted for use only in buyer's own youth group. This page can be downloaded from the Web site for this book: www.YouthSpecialties.com/store/downloads   password: dares2
Copyright © 2003 by Youth Specialties.

An area of my life where i need more faith...

My prayer for faith

My Mountain, My Sea

An area of my life where i need more faith...

My prayer for faith

From *Wild Truth Bible Lessons—Dares from Jesus 2* by Mark Oestreicher. Permission to reproduce this page granted for use only in buyer's own youth group.
This page can be downloaded from the Web site for this book: www.YouthSpecialties.com/store/downloads   password: dares2
Copyright © 2003 by Youth Specialties.

Give 'Til it Hurts

"As he looked up, Jesus saw the rich putting their gifts into the temple treasury. He also saw a poor widow put in two very small copper coins. 'I tell you the truth,' he said, 'this poor widow has put in more than all the others. All these people gave their gifts out of their wealth; but she out of her poverty put in all she had to live on.'"

Luke 21:1-4

GOALS

STUDENTS WILL—

- Understand what generous giving looks like, and why Jesus cares about it
- Brainstorm ways teens can be generous givers
- Choose a plan of action to be a generous giver this week

GIVE AWAY

Pass out blank paper, and ask students to list their 10 most valuable possessions. Tell them that the items don't really have to belong to them (maybe their parents own the item), but they need to be the primary user of the item. For instance, they could list their bedroom. Or they could list the family TV, if they really use it more than anyone else in the house. But their lists might also include personal possessions, like a CD collection, a bike, or a special piece of jewelry. The items don't have to be in any particular order—just get 10 items listed. (If you're tight on time, you might consider shortening this list to five or seven items.)

YOU'LL NEED

- blank paper and pens or pencils for each student

Now start a process of whittling those items away! Say—**If you decided the best thing you could do would be to give one of those items away (not sell it; not have it taken from you), which would you choose?** Eventually, you'll get to the point where your

students think of giving all these items away; but at this point, that shouldn't be clear. Allow them to think first of those items on their list that have less value to them. Tell them to put a number One next to the item they chose to give away.

Ask—**How difficult would that be? What difference would it make in your life?**

Now continue the process by stating the question again—**If you decided the best thing you could do would be to give *another* one of those items away (not sell it; not have it taken from you), which would you choose? Put a number Two next to that item.** Ask the follow up questions again.

If you don't have much time—or if the students are responding well to the questions (which means the exercise will take much more time), you'll want to combine a handful of numbers at some point. Say something like—**okay, now choose the next five items you'll give away.** Continue in this manner all the way to the last item on everyone's list (until everyone has a "number nine" listed on their sheets, and one item that hasn't been given away). If your group is 20 or fewer kids, have everyone share what that item is. If your group is larger, ask for a dozen or so responses.

Ask—

• **Would it just seem totally crazy if I asked you to consider giving that last item away? Why or why not?**
• **What would it cost you—really—to give that away (not in money, but in results)?**

As difficult as it might be, try not to comment much on their responses at this point (if you're like me, you'll want to say things like, "C'mon, it's just a video game system!" and "I think you'd survive without your bedroom!" and "You know, First Church down the street has a great youth group you might want to check out."). Remember, these opening exercises are just to get kids thinking. This one is somewhat of a set-up, of course, as they've yet to see the dare from Jesus to be radical givers.

THE BUILDING CAMPAIGN

Recruit six volunteers (students or adult leaders) to play parts in a spontaneous melodrama. They don't have to learn lines or prepare a drama—they just have to be willing to play their parts with gusto. You'll need volunteers for these characters—
• The pastor
• The Building Campaign chairperson
• A rich guy and his wife
• A homeless guy
• The truth-teller

YOU'LL NEED

🦉 six volunteer actors to play parts in a spontaneous melodrama and Bibles

It's crucial that actors who can ad-lib some lines play the roles of the pastor and the building campaign chairperson. Not many of your kids will be capable of this—so either make sure you choose an extremely verbal kid who's comfortable up front, or assign these roles to adult volunteers. You will be the narrator. When you read anything with action, the actors should play out what you've said. When you read a line of dialogue, the actors should repeat the lines in character. Set up the scene, and instruct the rest of the group that they are the congregation, and they

will have a handful of responses to play also.

Now read the script, pausing at appropriate times for action or lines. If a character has a multi-sentence part to speak, pause between each sentence for them to repeat the line before you continue.

After the drama (I use this term very loosely!) has concluded, ask for a round of applause for the incredible acting of this talented group of thespians (ooh—careful with that word).

If your group has kids who are familiar with the stories of the Bible, ask—**Does this story sound familiar to anyone?** If anyone answers yes, ask—**Why? Where have you heard it before?** Of course, it's a modernized version of the story of Jesus noticing the poor widow who gave two copper coins to the temple, and the Truth-Teller said something very similar to what Jesus said in his dare.

If your group is *not* familiar with the stories of the Bible, say something like—**This story is in the Bible—with a few different details.**

Have kids turn in their Bibles (make sure everyone can see one) to Luke 21:1-4, and read it to your group—

> *"As he looked up, Jesus saw the rich putting their gifts into the temple treasury. He also saw a poor widow put in two very small copper coins. "I tell you the truth," he said, "this poor widow has put in more than all the others. All these people gave their gifts out of their wealth; but she out of her poverty put in all she had to live on."*

Then lead a discussion with these questions—
• **What did the poor widow give?** *Two small copper coins, or everything she had to live on.*
• **Why was this a big deal, even though it was a very small amount?** *It was everything she had!*
• **Does it seem foolish for a poor lady to give almost everything she has, rather than taking care of her own needs first? Why or why not?** *On one level, it does seem foolish! How's she going to live if she gives all her money away? But—of course—Jesus is clearly praising this woman, saying that her faith and generosity are what pleases God, not the size of the gift.*

- **Would our culture say the lady was being irresponsible? Why or why not?** *Yes, many would say—even in our churches—that she was being irresponsible. People might say she was not being wise with the small amount of money she had.*
- **What did Jesus say about her gift?** *It was the bigger gift, compared to the gifts of the rich people.*
- **What was wrong with the gifts of the rich people, compared to her gift?** *Their gifts didn't require any sacrifice.*
- **Why does Jesus want us to give so much? Is God so poor that he needs everything we have?** *Of course, this last idea is silly. God doesn't need our resources. But this is a very difficult question for teens. Allow them to struggle with it for a bit—don't just provide the right answer immediately. There are a couple issues here. First, when we give like the poor widow, we prove our dependence on God rather than on ourselves. Focusing on giving, rather than on our own stuff, keeps our priorities in the right place. Also, we need to realize that in God's great love for us, he knows that this kind of living will make us happier, healthier people. Tiny giving usually feels like an obligation. Real sacrificial giving usually feels just crazy enough to cause us to reflect on the ultimate giver: Jesus.*
- **How did Jesus give generously to us?** *He gave us life! And he gave his own life so we could be reconnected to God!*

Wrap up this section by saying something like— **Jewish people, in the Bible, were told to give 10 percent—often called a** *tithe.* **Today, many churches still hold this up as an expectation. But Jesus blows this away by daring people to give sacrificially—not just by a percentage.**

Most young teens think of giving only in terms of giving money to the church in the offering plate. And most young teens don't have

much to give in that sense. It's important that you help them expand this dare beyond giving money to church. This is about being a giving person; and teens have lots of other stuff to give besides money.

Ask kids to brainstorm things they can give, and write the list of items they think of on a board or large piece of paper. This could include things like—

YOU'LL NEED

- a board or large piece of paper

- Money
- Time
- Attention
- Respect
- Obedience
- Service
- Love
- Encouragement

(All these items are on the final application handout)

Once you have a good list compiled, go back over the list one item at a time, asking students to give examples of what giving this item—giving like the poor widow, not like the rich people—would look like for a teen.

For example, when you talk about giving money, help kids think through the fact that many of them could be more like the poor widow than the rich people. They don't have much money to give. So when they give it generously, their gift is actually much larger than someone who gives thousands of dollars.

Also push them to give examples of giving money beyond just putting a couple bucks in an offering plate. Where else could they give money?

Go through this process—allowing kids to brainstorm in third-person examples for each giving item on the list. (It's usually easier for teens to think about third-person applications than to think of first-person applications.)

Take your time with this process; don't rush it. It's the key to your students understanding and applying this dare. Our goal is not to create kids who tip God as they would a waitress, but kids who understand true sacrificial giving in every area of life.

Pass out copies of **My Generous Gift** (Wildpage 9.1) and pens or pencils to each perfect little angel (and the rest of the group also). Point out that the sheet has a list of ways teens

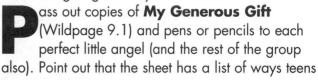

MY GENEROUS GIFT

can give—similar to the list they just brainstormed.

And similar to the way they just brainstormed, they should take a few minutes on their own to think of a couple ways they could actually *do* something this week to give generously. Tell them to make sure their plans are specific—not things like "I'll give more money." Instead they should write things like, "This week I'll call the nursery coordinator about volunteering to help every other Sunday in the church nursery." Or, "This week I could make a whole bunch of sandwiches and take them to the homeless people in the park."

After a few minutes for students to write plans of action, encourage them to take the final action step and circle the plan they are committing to carry out this week. Ask if a few would be willing to share their plans with the whole group.

Then close in prayer, thanking Jesus for his life-changing sacrifice for us, and asking for strength to live out this dare.

YOU'LL NEED

ග copies of **Wildpage 9.1** and pens or pencils for each student

The Building Campaign

Characters:
- The Pastor (must be played by someone who can ad-lib)
- The Building Campaign chairperson (some ad-libbing required)
- A rich guy and his wife
- A homeless guy
- The truth-teller

Scene: A church service. All students without assigned roles are part of the congregation. Pastor stands at the front. The homeless guy sits in the back row.

Welcome to church! The service has just begun. The opening music has faded away, and the pastor begins the service by welcoming the congregation and making his usual remarks.

(Pause for the pastor to make up some comments.)

Now the pastor announces that the church is about to launch a big new building campaign, raising millions of dollars to build a new sanctuary. He describes the vision for the new facility, an incredible new place with all the latest technology.

(Pause for the pastor to talk about the new building and the money needed.)

The pastor invites the building campaign chairperson to the front, makes an introduction, and allows the chairperson to share more about the vision. The chairperson could not be more excited about this new building and talks with weird exaggeration about how important this is for the future of the church.

(Pause for chairperson to be weird and pitch the building idea.)

The chairperson announces, "This morning we'll be taking pledges—publicly. We think it's important to make our giving known to each other—to challenge each other to greater sacrifice! I'd like to start this process by inviting our rich guy and his wife to come to the front."

The rich guy and his wife make their way to the front of the church. Both of them seem like they are dripping with money. He is a jerk, who loves to be the big man and talk about how rich he is. She absolutely loves all this attention. The rich guy says, "As you all know, I've been blessed with lots and lots of money. You've all been to our incredible house, which makes all of your houses look like a joke. You've all seen our Mercedes. You've all seen our expensive jewelry and super-fine clothes."

The wife pipes in, with a big cheesy smile on her face, "...it's not always easy living with so much money—sometimes we are asked to give some away!"

The rich guy continues, "So we've decided to make a big difference in this building campaign. We're going to give $100,000!"

The congregation gasps. Everyone starts murmuring about how much money that is. The wife says, "Yes, that sure is a lot of money! But we just want it to be clear that we're really, really giving people. And we're very spiritual."

The pastor smiles. The campaign chairperson smiles and smacks the rich guy on the back in

From *Wild Truth Bible Lessons—Dares from Jesus 2* by Mark Oestreicher. Permission to reproduce this page granted for use only in buyer's own youth group. This page can be downloaded from the Web site for this book: www.YouthSpecialties.com/store/downloads   password: dares2
Copyright © 2003 by Youth Specialties.

playful affirmation, then asks, "Who will be next? Who will come forward and make their pledge?"

There's a homeless guy in the back row. No one can stand that this guy even comes to the church. No one sits near him because he smells and wears really dirty clothes. He doesn't shave, and he basically looks like a mess! But suddenly he stands. The congregation gasps again and begins to murmur about the man.

With his head low, he shuffles to the front of the church. Everyone up front (the pastor, the campaign chairperson, and especially the rich guy and his wife) look horrified. They back away, not wanting any contact with the man. When the man gets to the front, he hands something to the campaign chair.

The campaign chair says very loudly, "A dollar? You're giving a dollar?"

The congregation gasps again. The rich guy and his wife begin laughing—a loud obnoxious arrogant laugh. The wife says, "Can you believe this guy? He stinks up our church! Then he comes forward after our HUGE gift, and gives a dollar?! How absurd!"

Just then, the Truth-Teller stands in the midst of the congregation and silences everyone. The Truth-Teller says, "What's wrong with you people?"

The congregation gasps again.

The Truth-Teller continues, "Don't you see? These rich people—they gave out of their wealth, and their gift is rather puny and wimpy. But this man, he gave everything he has! His gift is so much bigger than theirs!"

The congregation gasps one more time. The campaign chair and the pastor grumble. The rich guy grits his teeth. The rich wife faints to the floor.

And now, the congregation breaks into cheers!

From *Wild Truth Bible Lessons—Dares from Jesus 2* by Mark Oestreicher. Permission to reproduce this page granted for use only in buyer's own youth group. This page can be downloaded from the Web site for this book: www.YouthSpecialties.com/store/downloads   password: dares2
Copyright © 2003 by Youth Specialties.

My Generous Gift

9.1

Look over the list below of ways to give. Choose one or two that you will accept as a dare this week. Then write a giving plan (be specific—give details) for generous giving in that area this week. Circle what you wrote, if you're willing to Take the Dare!

Money

Time

Attention

Respect

Obedience

Service

Love

Encouragement

Other

69

From *Wild Truth Bible Lessons—Dares from Jesus 2* by Mark Oestreicher. Permission to reproduce this page granted for use only in buyer's own youth group.
This page can be downloaded from the Web site for this book: www.YouthSpecialties.com/store/downloads   password: dares2
Copyright © 2003 by Youth Specialties.

The Big Dare

"For God so loved the world that he gave his one and only Son, that whoever believes in him shall not perish but have eternal life. For God did not send his Son into the world to condemn the world, but to save the world through him. Whoever believes in him is not condemned, but whoever does not believe stands condemned already because he has not believed in the name of God's one and only Son."

John 3:16-18

GOALS

STUDENTS WILL—

- Understand Jesus' dare to believe
- Consider *what and who* they are being dared to believe in
- Write a personal statement of belief

BELIEVE IT OR NOT (EPISODE TWO)

Yeah, yeah, we played a believe-it-or-not game a few lessons back (if you're teaching these things in the order they appear in the book—which is not necessary, by the way). So sue me. This is just such a perfect place for another one, since it's a lesson on believing! And it's really a very different game.

YOU'LL NEED

- Copies of Wildpage 10.1 (**Believe It or Not Tombstones**) and one pen or pencil for each team. Or see the no-handout options in the sidebar.
- Optional: a small candy prize for the winning team

Break your group into teams (of any size, really—five to eight seems to work well for this kind of game). Hand out copies of **Believe It or Not Tombstones** (Wildpage 10.1), and give one pen or pencil to each team.

Explain (as it says at the top of the Wildpage) that people used to inscribe things on the tombstones (grave markers). Often these were simple sayings (as are still common today), such as *Beloved*

Husband and Father or *Rest in Peace*. But sometimes they got a little wordier. The list on the Wildpage contains both real tombstone inscriptions (found on tombstones around North America) as well as fakes (straight out of my twisted little pea brain). Each team should discuss each inscription, then decide together whether to check the "Believe it!" box, or the "Don't Believe it!" box next to each item. Give them a fairly short time limit to complete this—about three minutes should do it.

Go through the first 10 inscriptions (save the bonus question), and have teams shout out their answers. Then have teams total up their correct answers before moving on to the bonus question. The bonus question is a tricky little device I use to level the playing field. Assign enough points to the bonus question so a good percentage of the teams still have a chance to make a comeback if they get it right. For example, if the leading team has nine correct answers prior to the bonus question, and most of the other teams have six to eight right, make the bonus question worth four points. The team in the lead may whine and groan. Hey, there's a great spiritual principle there (think "thief on the cross next to Jesus" or Jesus' parable of the workers in the field)

if you want to explore it. Consider awarding a small candy prize to the winning team.

Note: As with any game or teaching idea, use a little sensitivity. If you have a kid in your group who just had someone very close to them die, save this game for another time!

No handout options.

This game really doesn't require a handout. It's just that reading the inscriptions will help some students. Here are two other options—

• **PowerPoint or MediaShout game.** In my junior high group, I would run the game this way. Put each of the inscriptions on a PowerPoint or MediaShout slide. Don't reveal the answers the first time you go through them. Give each team a blank piece of paper and have them write "Believe it!" or "Don't Believe It!" next to the first 10 tombstone inscriptions. Hold off on the bonus question on the first pass. (Don't even let them know there *is* a bonus question.) Keep the time for deciding each response fairly short (30 seconds or so). Then go back through the list a second time (you'll need a second series of slides in your presentation), and have the teams shout out their answers, before "Believe it!" or "Don't Believe It!" pops up over the inscription on the slide. After the first 10 questions, have the teams total up their correct responses, and find out which team is in the lead. Then reveal that there's a bonus round. Make the points for the bonus round worth enough so that about half the teams are still in the running to win if they get it correct.
• **Audible game.** Just read the inscriptions to the teams (you'll probably need to read each one a couple of times), and have students write, "Believe it!" or "Don't Believe It!" on their blank sheets as above. Hold off on the bonus question as above, until the first 10 have been scored.

Here are the answers—
• **Here lies Johnny Yeast. Pardon me for not rising.** *"Believe it!"*
• **I was somebody. Who is no business of yours.** *"Believe it!"*
• **Ada, Alice, and Agnes, triplets forever. One** of them is here; guess nothing lasts forever. *"Don't believe it!"*
• **I told you I was sick!** *"Believe it!"*
• **Here lies Timmy, my little brother, even tho' he was 92. At least I'm not the older brother anymore.** *"Don't believe it!"*
• **Margaret Daniels: She always said her feet were killing her, but nobody believed her.** *"Believe it!"*
• **Here lies the body of our Anna**
Done to death by a banana.
It wasn't the fruit that laid her low
But the skin of the thing that made her go. *"Believe it!"*
• **"Blast it all!" That's what Charles said before he lit the fuse.** *"Don't believe it!"*
• **Here lies Gullible Pete. It was Stanley who told him he could fly off that cliff.** *"Don't believe it!"*
• **Harry Edsel Smith of Albany, New York: Born 1903—Died 1942. Looked up the elevator shaft to see if the car was on the way down. It was.** *"Believe it!"*
Bonus question:
• **I really liked my life. Too bad I liked bears too.** *"Don't believe it!"*

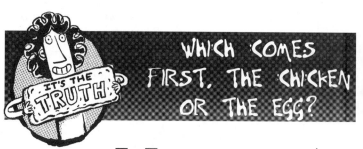

WHICH COMES FIRST, THE CHICKEN OR THE EGG?

Have your teams stay together for a few more minutes, and make a transition by asking these questions—

• **What is belief?** *Don't push for a right answer—or your definition of a right answer—at this point. Just get some ideas expressed.*
• **What role does belief play in being a Jesus-follower?** *It plays a HUGE role! Without belief, or faith, we'd be left with just a list of good ideas for living. Belief is what makes us Jesus-followers!*

YOU'LL NEED

ö Bibles, or some other way to show the scripture you'll use

Now say something like—**I'm sure you've all heard the famous question: Which came first, the chicken or the egg? In your teams, take a minute to think of other similar questions about the order of things. See if you can come up with a few more. Have someone on your team write down any ideas you come up with.**

After giving the teams a few minutes, have them read their answers. They may come up with questions like—
• *Did Adam and Eve have belly buttons?*
• *Which comes first, an acorn or an oak tree?*
• Or even, *which comes first, summer vacation or a school year?*

Then ask this one—**Which comes first, belief or understanding?** Clarify the question with an explanation along these lines—**Do you think the normal order is that we learn and start to understand things about God, and then we can have belief? Or, is it the other way around: we have belief first, and then start to understand things about God?**

Let your group wrestle with this a bit. Hopefully you'll have some dissenting views and can stir up a bit of conversation around this question. If your kids are fairly nonresponsive, take the lead and point out that most people probably think of the answer to that question as—We have to understand certain things about God and how he works in order to have faith, in order to believe.

Now have students look in their Bibles at the second half of Isaiah 7:9 (*"If you do not stand firm in your faith, you will not stand at all."*). Say something like—**Another way of saying this is—If you don't believe, you won't understand. If we try to have total understanding about God and following him, then what follows isn't really belief; it's more like legal proof. Instead, we have to take the risky step of believing first! Then—and only then, according to the Bible—God will help us to understand more and more as we spend time with him.**

Now have students turn in their Bibles to the dare for today. It's a pretty familiar passage to any kid who's grown up around the church at all: John 3:16. It's the granddaddy of all dares! After reading it, ask your group what they think the dare from Jesus is in this passage. (It should be fairly clear after the mini-talk you've just given about belief and understanding.) If your question is met with blank stares and silence (welcome to young teen ministry!), clarify by asking—**Is Jesus daring us to understand more?** *No.* **Is Jesus daring us to believe?** *Yes. (Duh.)*

Continue your discussion with these questions—
• **Why would Jesus dare us to believe?** *Belief is a choice that not everyone makes. It's even kind of a risky choice.*
• **How can we know what to believe and what not to believe?** *This is a tough one. Obviously, we have to use some discernment and wisdom. For most of us, we knew or felt or experienced enough about God to make the choice to follow him a reasonable one. Not that following God is about reason! In the end, this is an important role of the Holy Spirit, to help us use wisdom in what we believe and don't believe.*
• **Whether you're already a Christian or not, what difference would it make in your life if you** *really* **believed and lived out that God loves you as Jesus says in the dare verse?**

IS SHE TAKING THE DARE?

This is going to be tricky, but let's give it a shot together (You're thinkin', "Yeah, you're not the one standing in front of my group!"). God reveals his truth in lots of ways (you'll get to this), but that doesn't mean we want to piece together a faith system, a set of beliefs, from anywhere and everywhere. Of course, this is extremely common today; and you'd be surprised how many of your

YOU'LL NEED
⬥ a whiteboard or large piece of paper

kids have belief systems that are a hodgepodge (did I just write hodgepodge?) of different ideas. So, begin by asking your students to brainstorm a list of ways that God makes truths known to us—how does he help us know him and his desires? Write the list on a whiteboard or large piece of paper. It might include things like—

- The Bible
- Nature
- Other Christ-followers
- Our conscience
- The Holy Spirit
- The church and other spiritual leaders
- In our thinking and hearts

Spend a bit of time on this list. Explain that these sources become inputs for our beliefs—like a water tap is a source for water, these sources fuel our beliefs. Go over the list item by item, and ask kids to decide if that item is a way they build their beliefs or not. Discuss why or why not.

Then tell the group you're going to add to the list a bit. Draw a line below the last item on the current list, and then add these items—

- Buddhism
- Astrology (horoscopes)
- Wicca

Ask, "What are other things people look to for truth or beliefs?" Have kids add to this new list.

Caution: this is *not* a lesson on "icky evil stuff to stay away from." Our goal here is not to demonize other faiths or turn this lesson into a witch-hunt. Your goal in listing these other belief systems is to talk about sources of truth and belief with your group.

Now read this first-person testimony—**My name is Stacey. I've been going to church all my life. I totally believe in God, and that Jesus saves me. But lately, I've been finding that's there are lots of different places to find truth. My friend gave me this book about Buddhism, and I was kinda surprised to find all kinds of great stuff in it. The way I see it is, maybe there are lots of ways to find truth, lots of ways to believe. And maybe God is behind them all in some way.**

Ask—
- **What is the dare this week?** *To believe in Jesus.*
- **Is Stacey taking the dare?** *Your group will undoubtedly have some kids who will quickly answer, 'No.' But you will likely have others who think Stacey is pursuing truth, and that's a good thing—they just won't be willing to share it in your group if they think you'll come down on them. Try to get some discussion going on this question—use these follow-up questions if needed.*
- **What's good about what Stacey is doing?** *Well, she's actually looking for truth—looking for things to fuel her belief. This is good.*
- **What's risky about what Stacey is doing?** *It can be easy to assume that because she finds some good things in Buddhism, that it must all be true.*
- **Then how do we really take this dare?** *Have students look at John 3:16 again if they're not sure how to answer this question. The key is Jesus. The dare isn't to have beliefs. Everyone has beliefs. The dare is to believe in Jesus. And we can't really say we believe in Jesus unless we're willing to follow him and live what he says.*

WHAT DO I BELIEVE?

Wrap up this lesson by giving kids time—probably in small groups, but on their own would work in some groups—to write statements of belief. Their statements can be a list of sentences, or they can be in paragraph form. It might be helpful to have your church's statement of faith as an example—so kids can see what one looks like. If they're still fairly clueless about how to proceed, give them categories. Have them write out their belief about God, about Jesus, about the Holy Spirit, about the Church, and about Christian living (or something like that).

YOU'LL NEED

ỗ Blank paper and writing utensils

If your church is part of a tradition that memorizes or repeats a catechism or creed (like the Apostles Creed) on a regular basis—enough that your kids would be very familiar with it—then consider giving your kids a copy of that statement, and having them rewrite it in their own words, instead of making something up from scratch.

After everyone has a chance to write a statement, read them to each other. If you hear anything truly aberrant, you may want to stop and ask a question about it.

Remind your group that living out this dare means looking to Jesus as the source of all our beliefs, as the source of all truth. Challenge your students to be aware of how Jesus will reveal himself to them this week.

Close your time in prayer, thanking God for helping us find truth. Pray for wisdom to know what is and isn't true—what deserves our belief and what doesn't.

People sometimes have little messages inscribed on tombstones (this was very common years ago). For each of the tombstone inscriptions below, check either the "Believe it!" or the "Don't Believe it!" box.

I believe it! / I don't believe it!

❑ ❑ Here lies Johnny Yeast. Pardon me for not rising.

❑ ❑ I was somebody. Who is no business of yours.

❑ ❑ Ada, Alice and Agnes, triplets forever. One of them is here; guess nothing lasts forever.

❑ ❑ I told you I was sick!

❑ ❑ Here lies Timmy, my little brother, even tho' he was 92. At least I'm not the older brother anymore.

❑ ❑ Margaret Daniels: She always said her feet were killing her, but nobody believed her.

❑ ❑ Here lies the body of our Anna
Done to death by a banana.
It wasn't the fruit that laid her low
But the skin of the thing that made her go.

❑ ❑ "Blast it all!" That's what Charles said before he lit the fuse.

❑ ❑ Here lies Gullible Pete. It was Stanley who told him he could fly off that cliff.

❑ ❑ Harry Edsel Smith of Albany, New York: Born 1903—Died 1942. Looked up the elevator shaft to see if the car was on the way down. It was.

Bonus Round!

❑ ❑ I really liked my life. Too bad I liked bears too.

76

From *Wild Truth Bible Lessons—Dares from Jesus 2* by Mark Oestreicher. Permission to reproduce this page granted for use only in buyer's own youth group.
This page can be downloaded from the Web site for this book: www.YouthSpecialties.com/store/downloads   password: dares2
Copyright © 2003 by Youth Specialties.

Show the Sign

"A new command I give you: Love one another. As I have loved you, so you must love one another. By this all men will know that you are my disciples, if you love one another."

John 13:34-35

GOALS

STUDENTS WILL—

- Learn that loving one another should be the distinguishing mark of Christians
- Discuss implications of their youth group being loving to each other
- Agree to a group application of holding each other accountable to love

HUG TAG

Oh man, some of you guys will rebel against this game! That's part of what makes it so perfect as an opener for this lesson.

Play a game of tag (really, you can use almost any set of tag rules you like). But instead of merely touching people to tag them, whoever is *IT* has to hug them. The person getting tagged can try to not get caught, of course. But once caught, they're not allowed to resist the hug.

YOU'LL NEED

- nothing but space

I would play it this way: one person begins as the hugger. Every person he hugs also becomes a hugger. Last person gets a big group hug in the middle of a bunch of people. This will, most likely, be a very quick game. So you might want to play it more than once.

If your group was good at this game and didn't get all weirded out by the hugging thing, move right on to the next part of the lesson. But if the hugging was obviously awkward for at least a portion of the group, ask these questions—

- **Why did the hugging part seem awkward?** *The answer for most kids would be that they aren't used to being intimately physical with people—and hugging expresses care, which many of them aren't ready to express to the people they had to hug. But they would probably say that like this, "Because it was weird!"*

- ***Should* it seem awkward or weird?** *Not really, not in the context of our group—it's not as if you were walking up to total strangers on the street and hugging them.*

WHAT'S THE DIFFERENCE?

Don't reveal the topic of the dare to your students yet, or it will steal the thunder from this exercise.

Pass out copies of **What's the Difference?** (Wildpage 11.1) to your students. (See "no handout options" in the sidebar for other ways to do this.) Ask if your students have ever done one of those games where they look at two almost-identical

YOU'LL NEED

- Bibles
- Optional: copies of Wildpage 11.1 **(What's the Difference?)** for each student

pictures and try to spot the differences. Then explain that this is a similar activity.

Read through the descriptions of the six groups. Encourage your group to listen for the differences. Explain that they shouldn't worry about the obvious differences, like names or location of meetings. They should look for the core differences: What is the group like? What is their goal? Why do they exist?

No Handout Options

The Wildpage on this exercise is really not totally necessary. It has a lot of content, so if your group would struggle to remember everything that's said about the groups, the handout will give them something to look at, and look back over as they think through the questions you'll ask. But you could—

- Pick students to represent each group. Put a sign around their necks with the name of the group they represent, and have them stand up front and read the description of their group. It would be best if you translated the descriptions into first person so it sounds as if the readers are part of the groups they're reading about.
- Use PowerPoint or MediaShout to project the key points of each group while you read the descriptions.
- Break your group into six teams (of any size), and give them one of the descriptions. Have them spend a couple minutes talking about their group, and then present themselves to the other groups.

Now lead a discussion with your group based on the primary question you've already asked them to watch for: what's the difference in these groups?

(Note: Admittedly, the youth group in this example is a bit idealized. Many church youth groups don't really function this way, and they are really more like a social group or like the Boys and Girls Clubs. But the description of the church youth group is what a church youth group *should* be! Here's a little challenge for you: if your group is just about Christian education, you're missing the point.)

Your group should see the difference without you pointing it out: that the church youth group has a lot of similarities to the other groups, but it should be a place of love. (Your kids won't use that language.) It should be a place where group members accept each other and care about each other—where their primary function is to love each other and to help each other love God and experience God's love.

Now have kids turn in their Bibles to the dare for this lesson (or make the passage visible in some other way). Read Jesus' dare from John 13:34-35: *"A new command I give you: Love one another. As I have loved you, so you must love one another. By this all men will know that you are my disciples, if you love one another."*

Lead a discussion with these questions—
- **In this dare, is Jesus challenging us to love everyone in the world?** *No. While that is a consistent message in the Bible—and in Jesus' teaching—that is not what he's saying here. He's daring us to love each other. In other words, to love other Christians.*
- **Why would Jesus focus a dare just on how Christians treat other Christians? Doesn't that seem to leave out the rest of the world?** *The answer to this question is right in the verse: if we really love each other, our love will be attractive to others. People will know that what we believe is real by observing how we treat each other.*
- **What does it mean to love each other? Does that mean we should all be *in love*?** *No. Loving each other means caring for each other, treating each other with respect, and lots of other stuff.*

TRUTH in ACTION

LOVING YOU....

Have students turn in their Bibles to 1 Corinthians:13, and read verses 4 through 8a (the primary chunk of the love chapter). Then read this first-person plural paraphrase, referring to your group—**When we are patient with each other, we show love. When we are kind to each**

other, we prove love. If we love each other, we won't be jealous of each other, we won't be braggers, and we won't be proud or stuck-up. If we are a loving group, we won't be rude to each other, we won't be selfish, we won't get angry at each other, and we won't hold grudges. We'll focus on truth. We'll protect each other, trust each other, believe in each other, and not give up. If we love each other, it will last.

YOU'LL NEED

ठ Bibles

Have a discussion around these questions (don't rush this part—this is the core application brainstorming time in the lesson)—

• **How well does that describe our group?** Talk about this for a while.
• **What actions can we take to become closer to this description?** Brainstorm a big list, if possible.
• **What actions tear down that goal?** Brainstorm another big list.

UNHOSLTER THE U

Most of the dares in this book of lessons have individual action points. But since this seems to be a group dare, this is a group application. It's a semi-goofy little reminder I used for years in one church youth group where we struggled with this issue. And despite its goofiness, it really made a difference over time, as kids were regularly reminded of this goal.

YOU'LL NEED

ठ Your hands. Hopefully that won't be a problem for you.

Tell your group you're going to teach them a little hand motion, then tell them how and when to use it. Hold your right hand (oh, stop whining left-handed people!) on your hip, with your hand forming a big letter "U." Then whip your hand out in front of you in your best gunslinger impersonation, and say: **Unity begins with U!**

Point out the obvious: Yes, the word unity begins with the letter *U*. But more than that, we'll never experience love and unity in our group if we wait for others to make it happen. It has to start with *you*.

Perform the action again, while saying the phrase. Then have your group stand up and practice the action (with the phrase) several times.

Have them sit back down and explain that the dare is for them to "Unholster the U"—to be aware of times when the love commitment we just talked about is threatened or violated. For instance, if they hear gossip, they should "Unholster the U" to communicate that they think it's destructive to love in the group. If someone is putting someone down, "Unholster the U." They can even unholster the U to themselves if they catch themselves in the midst of some action or conversation that is destructive to love.

Ask the group if they're willing to take this dare to live out love as a group. Then ask if they're willing to try unholstering the U for a while, to see if it acts as a good reminder to each other.

Have them practice the motion and phrase one more time. If your group can handle it, it would be funny to end your time by having everyone give out hugs to five people each.

Close your time in prayer, asking God to help your group become the kind of loving group talked about in the dare, and in 1 Corinthians 13; that other teenagers, and even adults, would be able to see that this group is different because they really love each other.

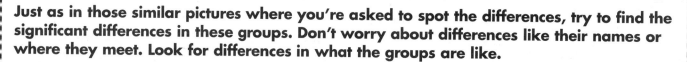

Just as in those similar pictures where you're asked to spot the differences, try to find the significant differences in these groups. Don't worry about differences like their names or where they meet. Look for differences in what the groups are like.

Group #1: The 4-H Club

This group meets after school in a small town, and it's mostly children of farmers. They learn stuff about raising animals and other farm-oriented topics. They work on projects, sometimes on their own and sometimes in teams. And they have lots of fun field trips and social gatherings. The goal of the group is to provide a place for kids to hang out and to teach them about farming and nature.

Group #2: Boy Scouts or Girl Scouts

These groups meet at various times but mostly in the evening. They play games and work on projects to earn merit badges for completing certain lists of things. They learn about all kinds of things like nature, science, and art. And they have camping trips and other fun activities in addition to their regular meetings. The goal of the group is to help kids develop good character and learn more about the world.

Group #3: Boys and Girls Club

Most Boys and Girls Clubs meet in urban settings where kids don't have as many options of positive groups to hang around with. They're kind of like Boy Scouts and Girl Scouts but without all the merit badges and stuff. They learn different things, and they work on projects together. They might get tutoring help with school homework, or talk about life issues. The goal of the group is to provide a safe place for kids to hang out and to help them succeed in life.

Group #4: The Church Youth Group

This group meets at different times but usually once or twice a week for social stuff and Bible study. They go on fun trips together and learn about God. They pray for each other and support each other in life. The goal of the group is to love each other and love God together.

Group #5: The School Science Club

This group meets after school one day a week in the science teacher's room. They talk about science and do cool experiments together. The goal of the group is to understand science better.

Group #6: The Soccer Team

Depending on how competitive they are, the team meets regularly for practice and also for games against other teams. At practices they work on different soccer skills as well as working as a team. The goal of the team is to give kids something positive to be a part of, to learn teamwork, and to play soccer.

80

From *Wild Truth Bible Lessons—Dares from Jesus 2* by Mark Oestreicher. Permission to reproduce this page granted for use only in buyer's own youth group.
This page can be downloaded from the Web site for this book: www.YouthSpecialties.com/store/downloads   password: dares2
Copyright © 2003 by Youth Specialties.

WILDPAGE

WILDPAGE

WILDPAGE

W I L D P A G E

Youth Group Love One Another Bookmarks

11.2

Our goal as a group:

When we are patient with each other, we show love. When we are kind to each other, we prove love. If we love each other, we won't be jealous of each other, we won't be braggers, and we won't be proud or stuck-up. If we are a loving group, we won't be rude to each other, we won't be selfish, we won't get angry at each other, and we won't hold grudges. We'll focus on truth. We'll protect each other, trust each other, believe in each other, and not give up. If we love each other, it will last.
From 1 Corinthians:13

Remember:
Unity begins with

U!

Our goal as a group:

When we are patient with each other, we show love. When we are kind to each other, we prove love. If we love each other, we won't be jealous of each other, we won't be braggers, and we won't be proud or stuck-up. If we are a loving group, we won't be rude to each other, we won't be selfish, we won't get angry at each other, and we won't hold grudges. We'll focus on truth. We'll protect each other, trust each other, believe in each other, and not give up. If we love each other, it will last.
From 1 Corinthians:13

Remember:
Unity begins with

U!

Our goal as a group:

When we are patient with each other, we show love. When we are kind to each other, we prove love. If we love each other, we won't be jealous of each other, we won't be braggers, and we won't be proud or stuck-up. If we are a loving group, we won't be rude to each other, we won't be selfish, we won't get angry at each other, and we won't hold grudges. We'll focus on truth. We'll protect each other, trust each other, believe in each other, and not give up. If we love each other, it will last.
From 1 Corinthians:13

Remember:
Unity begins with

U!

Our goal as a group:

When we are patient with each other, we show love. When we are kind to each other, we prove love. If we love each other, we won't be jealous of each other, we won't be braggers, and we won't be proud or stuck-up. If we are a loving group, we won't be rude to each other, we won't be selfish, we won't get angry at each other, and we won't hold grudges. We'll focus on truth. We'll protect each other, trust each other, believe in each other, and not give up. If we love each other, it will last.
From 1 Corinthians:13

Remember:
Unity begins with

U!

From *Wild Truth Bible Lessons—Dares from Jesus 2* by Mark Oestreicher. Permission to reproduce this page granted for use only in buyer's own youth group.
This page can be downloaded from the Web site for this book: www.YouthSpecialties.com/store/downloads   password: dares2
Copyright © 2003 by Youth Specialties.

Relax

"I have told you these things, so that in me you may have peace. In this world you will have trouble. But take heart! I have overcome the world."

John 16:33

GOALS

STUDENTS WILL—

- Understand the biblical concept of peace and that real peace can only be experienced in Jesus
- Discuss what it looks like for a young teen to *not* experience peace and to take steps toward experiencing peace
- Write and commit to a plan of action for experiencing more peace in their own lives

Say something like—**People talk about peace in many different ways. They use it to talk about different ideas. In this mixer, you'll see a few of those.**

Pass out copies of **Peace to You** (Wildpage 12.1) and pens or pencils to each student. Make sure they don't start until you've said, "Go." Read through the items (this will level the playing field a bit, as some kids would really struggle to read the sheet in the midst of the game). And make sure they understand the rules—especially that they can't get the same person's initials more than once (unless you have a small group and need to modify that rule). Also tell them that when they complete all the items, they should put their name on the top of the page and hand it to you.

YOU'LL NEED

✏ copies of Wildpage 12.1 (**Peace to You**) and pens or pencils for everyone

Now start the madness. To be honest, this mixer is quite contrary to peace, huh? (Screaming young teens running around your meeting room, yelling, "Peace" and staging mock sit-ins probably isn't quite what Jesus had in mind when he talked about peace! Peace, for you, might mean getting a substitute teacher!)

As the first few kids hand their completed sheets to you, check to see that they've actually completed everything, and that their names are on the top. End the game now, or—if you have time—let it continue on a bit longer so more kids will have time to complete additional items. Then have students return to their seats, and announce the winners. Consider awarding some kind of small prize (a candy bar, a new Lexus) to the first three finishers.

Even More Active Option: Slo-Mo Tag

Play a game of tag (you can use any set of rules you want). Except everyone must move in slow motion. Anyone caught moving at normal speed (or even fudging on their slo-mo and speeding it up a little to tag or avoid being tagged) will be eliminated. You'll need to be the judge of who gets eliminated for speeding.

THE ULTIMATE PEACE SIGN

Make a transition by asking these questions—

• **What is peace? What are some of the different things people mean when they use that word?** *There are many definitions, from lack of war to calm. Try to surface as many definitions as you can from your group.*

• **Which of those definitions do you think is the most common way people use the word** *peace?* *Probably the most common usage is the idea of calm and quiet. But don't direct your group to this answer. Let them respond freely.*

YOU'LL NEED

☉ some way to show a large peace sign, and later a large cross (or copies of the two pages at the end of this lesson with those two images)
☉ Bibles

Hold up a copy of the Peace Sign at the end of this lesson, or make one visible in some other way (draw one on a whiteboard or large piece of paper, or project one using MediaShout or PowerPoint).

Lead a short discussion using these questions—

• **In the 1960s and '70s, this sign was used a lot to symbolize peace. What did people mean when they used this sign?** *Primarily, it was used as an anti-war symbol. Of course, your kids probably won't use this language, but they should be able to get the gist of it.*

• **"Peace in the land" or "Peace in the world" is a reasonable idea of peace and certainly something God wants for us! Why might this idea of peace not be the strongest, or most complete, way to talk about peace?** *Just let 'em brainstorm on this one.*

• **Do you think this was the kind of peace Jesus was talking about when he told people about peace? Why or why not?** *It might have included this idea; but Jesus was talking about a different kind of peace, a peace that each of us can experience on our own.*

• **What's the opposite of peace?** *War, anger,* stress, discontent, tension.

• **What does it look like for a person (as opposed to a country) to experience peace?** *Lack of stress, being content, having confidence in who they are.*

Now have kids turn in their Bibles to the dare for this lesson (or make the passage visible in some other way). Read John 16:33 (*"I have told you these things, so that in me you may have peace. In this world you will have trouble. But take heart! I have overcome the world."*).

Then continue your discussion with these questions—

• **What does Jesus mean when he uses the word peace in this verse?** *Again, don't be too focused on getting the right answer here—the next question will clarify the point.*

• **Which of these three sentences best describes what Jesus is talking about?**

> **"You can experience a life with no more problems in it if you follow me."**

> **"You'll still have problems, but with me you can experience peace in the middle of your problems."** *Of course, this is the closest parallel.*

> **"I told you to have peace; so get with it and start having it!"**

• **So, Jesus seems to say peace isn't about having an absence of problems. How, then, do we experience peace?** *It's likely your kids won't think of the answer to this question. Let them struggle with it for a bit, then point them back to a key phrase in the verse: "so that in me you may have peace." That's the key to answering this question. Rephrase the question if you need to, to help your students grasp the point of this phrase, that we can only experience real peace with Jesus—he's the source of all real peace.*

• **How does that work? How can we experience peace with Jesus?** *Again, this is really an observation question, in that the answer is right in the passage. It's the second half: "you'll still have problems in this world—but, hey, don't forget that I've overcome this world!"*

• **What does Jesus mean when he says he's overcome this world? And what role does that play in our experiencing peace?** *This is a* *rephrasing of the last question, just to check for understanding.*

Note about the Peace Sign: some Christians still have a very strong negative reaction to this peace sign. Some say it's a satanic image, with a broken cross, and such. For many, this was more about all the behavior associated with the culture that used the peace sign. Don't get distracted by this discussion here (with your kids or in your own thinking). You're not using the peace sign in a positive or negative way here—it's just to clarify a point about real peace, as opposed to the partial peace represented by this sixties-era symbol.

PEA·CE CHAPTERS

You've probably noticed by now (last lesson in the book, if you're doing them in order—which I sure don't care if you do!) that I like to use a lot of little stories about young teens and the dares. Let me explain why: This third step in all these lessons is what Larry Richards (back several decades ago!) called the *look* part of a teaching time. It answers the question: What does the Bible *mean* in the life context of a young teen? Before getting to the personal application step in the last part of the lesson, it's crucial that kids think about what this truth (or dare, as the case may be) looks like with junior high skin on it. Case studies and stories allow your students the opportunity to flesh this out.

YOU'LL NEED

☺ a copy of the *Peace Chapters* stories at the end of this lesson to read to your group. Or make three copies for volunteers to read

So, in this section, you'll lead your students through the stories of three young teens who are not experiencing peace in one way or another. Each story has three chapters, to allow some change to develop over time. And it gives you an opportunity, after each chapter, to debrief a bit about what's going on in this imaginary teen's life.

Read the first chapter of Paige's story (from the *Peace Chapters* pages at the end of this lesson); then stop. Ask your group to rate her level of peace. It should be fairly low! Feel free to add clarifying questions at this point also, if you want to make sure your kids are tracking with the story. For instance, after the last chapter of each story, there's a question about what the characters could do to experience more peace in their lives. You might consider asking this question after each chapter.

Continue on with each chapter, asking for follow-up ratings on the character's progress.

Notes on the three stories—
• Paige doesn't really get it. Her story, and her progress, doesn't reflect any understanding that real peace comes from God. So she's trying other ways of dealing with her stress, but they're not really working.
• Charles and Jenna understand the dare much more than Paige. Just be careful with Charles that you don't imply that dealing with tough stuff in life is a piece of cake. Remember, Jesus says very clearly, "You will still have problems in this world!" A handful of kids in your group may be dealing with tough issues like Charles. But *many* of your teens are probably like Jenna in one way or another: they're just not very content with life.

Character variation: instead of you just reading the three stories, recruit three student volunteers to play the parts of Paige, Charles, and Jenna. Either have them wear signs around their necks with their names, or just introduce them as these characters. Have the students each read their own characters' stories. But you still act as an emcee, and ask the debriefing questions between each chapter.

GIMME PEACE!

After the third-person discussion you've just completed, have students turn their attention to their own lives. Ask them to think about their own levels of peace.

Pass out blank 3 x 5 cards (or half sheets of blank paper), and have them rate themselves, just as they rated the characters in *Peace Chapters*. On a scale of 1 to 10, 1 = no peace at all, and 10 = tons of peace every day.

YOU'LL NEED

ʘ 3 x 5 cards (or blank paper) and pens or pencils

Then ask them to think about what keeps them from experiencing real peace in their lives. Maybe it's a specific issue, as with Paige or Charles. Or maybe they're more like Jenna. If your group is vocal and fairly open, ask them to share some of their thoughts (this would be best done in the context of a small group). Either way, ask them write some thoughts down on their cards.

Then ask them to turn their cards over and write a few action steps they can take to experience more peace in their own lives. Again, this could be a private exercise; or if your group is comfortable sharing, have several students share their action steps.

Finally, ask your students if they're willing to take this dare and put those action steps into practice this week. If they are, they should sign the card on the side where they wrote the action steps.

Encourage them not to throw the cards away, but to take them home and put them somewhere where they'll see it—in the corner of a mirror in their room or on a bedside table.

Close your time in prayer. Try using a complete-the-sentence prayer method (explain this to your group before starting). After you open the prayer, say something like—**God, the things in my life that keep me from experiencing your peace are....** Students should pray by completing the sentence out loud. Then pray—**God, help me to do these things to experience more peace this week....** Again, they should pray out loud some of their action steps.

optional closing: Passing of the Peace

Complete the following items in any order you want. Get initials by each one, as instructed. Remember, you can't get the same person's initials more than once.

Peace, baby. Hold up the peace sign (looks pretty much like a victory sign, with two fingers forming a V) to someone on the other side of the room (they can't be near you!). When they see you and flash the peace sign back at you, make your way over to them and have them initial here—_____

Rest in Peace. Get three other people to do this one with you. Have one person lay on the floor as if they're dead. Everyone else stands around them as if they're at a funeral. Everyone cries a little. You say, "May he rest in peace." Have two of the mourners initial here—_____

Quiet! Stand on a chair and shout, "Can't I get a little peace and quiet in here?" Have someone who heard you initial here—_____

Sit-in. In the sixties, war protest groups would sometimes stage sit-ins, where they sat somewhere in the way of others to get noticed. Get three other people to do this one with you. Sit on the floor in a little circle. Then begin to sing, "Give peace a chance!" over and over again. Just make up a tune for it. After you've sung it five or more times, have two of your fellow protesters initial here—_____

Whirled Peas. Act very confused. Stand on a chair and loudly ask, "Did someone say something about whirled peas?" Have someone who heard you initial here—_____

Passing of the Peace. Many churches have a time in their church services where they pass the peace. Some churches just call it greeting each other. Give someone a hug, or a kiss on the cheek, and say, "Peace be with you." The person should respond, "And also with you." Have that person initial here—_____

From *Wild Truth Bible Lessons—Dares from Jesus 2* by Mark Oestreicher. Permission to reproduce this page granted for use only in buyer's own youth group.
This page can be downloaded from the Web site for this book: www.YouthSpecialties.com/store/downloads   password: dares2
Copyright © 2003 by Youth Specialties.

From *Wild Truth Bible Lessons—Dares from Jesus 2* by Mark Oestreicher. Permission to reproduce this page granted for use only in buyer's own youth group.
This page can be downloaded from the Web site for this book: www.YouthSpecialties.com/store/downloads   password: dares2
Copyright © 2003 by Youth Specialties.

From *Wild Truth Bible Lessons—Dares from Jesus 2* by Mark Oestreicher. Permission to reproduce this page granted for use only in buyer's own youth group.
This page can be downloaded from the Web site for this book: www.YouthSpecialties.com/store/downloads   password: dares2
Copyright © 2003 by Youth Specialties.

W i L D P A G E

Peace Chapters

Paige

Chapter One

My friends call me "the stress puppy" 'cause I'm just tweaked about everything all the time. I worry about my grades like crazy and about everything else too! I sleep terribly, and I have lots of nervous habits—like biting my nails and stuff.

On a scale of 1 to 10 (1 = zero peace, 10 = lotsa peace), where is Paige?

Chapter Two

Okay, so I made some changes in my life, and things are getting better. I created a schedule for my homework, and when it's done, I'm trying to not think about it again. I read a book on stress management for teenagers, and it had some good ideas too. I'm biting my nails less.

On a scale of 1 to 10 (1 = zero peace, 10 = lotsa peace), where is Paige?

Chapter Three

Something's just not right. I'm doin' all this stuff to have more peace. And it does seem to be helping some— but not enough! My mom said it's just my personality to be a stress-puppy, but I hope that's not really true. I don't want to spend the rest of my life this way!

On a scale of 1 to 10 (1 = zero peace, 10 = lotsa peace), where is Paige?

What can Paige do to experience more peace?

Charles

Chapter One

Hey, it's not so much that I'm stressed like my friend Paige (she's a total stress puppy!). My thing is that I've got some pretty serious problems, like, my parents are splitting up, and my older sister is getting into some really bad stuff. It's not making me all twitchy like Paige; it's just got me really down. I guess you could say I'm kinda depressed—not in the send-me-to-a-loony-farm kind of way; just in a regular teenage I've-got-real-problems kind of way.

On a scale of 1 to 10 (1 = zero peace, 10 = lotsa peace), where is Charles?

Chapter Two

I read this verse in the Bible the other day about real peace being in Jesus. I'm not totally sure what *in Jesus* means; but it sounds like a big part of what I need. The verse also says that problems are normal, but that Jesus can deal with problems, or something like that. I'm going to spend some time thinking about this verse.

On a scale of 1 to 10 (1 = zero peace, 10 = lotsa peace), where is Charles?

90

From *Wild Truth Bible Lessons—Dares from Jesus 2* by Mark Oestreicher. Permission to reproduce this page granted for use only in buyer's own youth group.
This page can be downloaded from the Web site for this book: www.YouthSpecialties.com/store/downloads   password: dares2
Copyright © 2003 by Youth Specialties.

Chapter Three

I have to tell you, things are going a lot better for me. And it's not that my problems have gone away—my parents are still having major problems, and my sister is still really messed up. But somehow, in the middle of all that, I'm finding some peace. I guess you could say that I'm choosing to believe that Jesus knows my situation, and somehow, I'm finding some peace in that.

On a scale of 1 to 10 (1 = zero peace, 10 = lotsa peace), where is Charles?

What can Charles do to experience more peace?

Jenna

Chapter One

I don't have any real big problems, I suppose—at least not like Charles. And I'm not a stress-puppy like Paige. But I still don't know what it's like to have peace. My dad says I'm not content—which I think means that I'm kinda frustrated, in a small way, with life in general. I'm bugged by all the hatred in the world. I'm bugged by everyone's focus on making money and getting a great job. And on the other end, the lazy kids I know who just blow everything off and don't care about anything bug me too.

On a scale of 1 to 10 (1 = zero peace, 10 = lotsa peace), where is Jenna?

Chapter Two

So I started praying about this. I've not prayed a lot in the past—just when I have a big test at school or something. I don't feel like I know what I'm doing with this prayer thing; but I'm just kinda talking to God about it, about my—what was that word?—about my discontent.

On a scale of 1 to 10 (1 = zero peace, 10 = lotsa peace), where is Jenna?

Chapter Three

Hey, good news: this prayer thing seems to be working! I'm not really sure *how* it's working—but it does seem like the more I talk to God about the things in my life that bug me, they don't bug me quite as much. I mean, they still *bother* me, but they don't totally *bug* me. Does that make sense? Anyhow, I guess I have a sense that God cares about the same stuff I do, and that's changing my thinking a bit.

On a scale of 1 to 10 (1 = zero peace, 10 = lotsa peace), where is Jenna?

What can Jenna do to experience more peace?

91

From *Wild Truth Bible Lessons—Dares from Jesus 2* by Mark Oestreicher. Permission to reproduce this page granted for use only in buyer's own youth group.
This page can be downloaded from the Web site for this book: www.YouthSpecialties.com/store/downloads   password: dares2
Copyright © 2003 by Youth Specialties.

More go-anywhere books guaranteed to get teenagers thinking, talking and laughing!

Have You Ever...? ....ISBN 0310-22439-X
Name Your Favorite..............ISBN 0310-24197-9
Unfinished Sentences ....ISBN 0310-23093-4
What If...?............................ISBN 0310-20776-2
Would You Rather?...............ISBN 0310-20943-9

To find these and other YS resources...
Visit your local Christian bookstore
Order online at **www.YouthSpecialties.com/store**
Or call **1.800.776.8008**

Youth Specialties

Contributing to Christian family harmony isn't just bearable, it's cool!

There are lots of books about how parents need to understand their teens better—maybe you've seen them lying around your house! Now there's a book filled with interesting stories, practical information, *and specific action plans* to help you improve your relationship and communication with your parents.

ISBN 0310-25049-8

To find this and other StudentWare books—
Visit your local Christian bookstore
Order online at **www.YouthSpecialties.com/store**
Or call **1.800.776.8008**